Destiny
IN DISGUISE

Destiny

In Disguise

Lessons and Blessings in a Cancer Journey

The Things I Wished I Knew Before Cancer Disrupted My Life

Shannan Lewis

XULON PRESS

Xulon Press
2301 Lucien Way #415
Maitland, FL 32751
407.339.4217
www.xulonpress.com

Printed in the United States of America.

Paperback ISBN-13: 978-1-6322-1594-9
eBook ISBN-13: 978-1-6322-1595-6

I lovingly dedicate this book to:

My children and co-survivors, *Shanel Blair and Daniel Blair*
My parents, *Joyce Wallace and Clement Wallace*
My siblings, *Alecia Lewis and Othniel Lewis*
My constant caregivers and drivers, *Zaneen Thompson, LaTosha Cherry, Dawn Martin, Dotlyn Facey, Marcia Miller, Reshon Moore and Cathy Farmer-Kindell*
My Sisterhood, *Andrea Cunard, Arleen Sandra Valentine & Lisa Hoang*
I am grateful to everyone who cared enough to *pray, pen encouraging words, provide tangible blessings and share the gift of presence during and after the cancer journey.*

I wrote this book primarily for the **BRAVE WARRIORS** *who have been diagnosed with cancer, the ones who are boldly battling and the ones whose lives have been impacted or will be touched in some way because of someone's cancer diagnosis.*
I applaud and salute the **BRAVE WARRIORS** *who have survived cancer and the ones who supported them through the fight.*
I publicly honor my fellow **BRAVE WARRIORS** *('Sister'ing Through Cancer') who succumbed to their cancer diagnosis after I wrote this book.*
Rest in peace Lace Taylor and Michelle ChelleyRey Reynolds.

Most importantly, **I dedicate this to my Father God who has been my most consistent Caregiver, Confidante, Comforter, Covering and Companion. I hope with everything in me that I have made Him proud of me.**

Table of Contents

Foreword

My introduction to Shannan Lewis was as an undergraduate student in a course that I was teaching, and I soon found her to be an intelligent, well-spoken, and vivacious lady with a charming Jamaican accent. It was gratifying to observe her development as a student and as a leader among her peers. Subsequently, I had her as a graduate student and then as a colleague when she began teaching at Palm Beach Atlantic University. Our conversations and discussions have always been insightful, and I am constantly learning from her.

When Shannan began her cancer journey, it was initially evident that this would be a faith journey for her. She poignantly expresses this in the triumphs, the challenges, and the struggles she encountered during this arduous pilgrimage. She allows us into her innermost thoughts and emotions as she had to deal with the diagnosis, the treatment, and the outcome. We walk with her through the difficult reality of being diagnosed with cancer and determining how to respond to such devastating news. With the diagnosis Shannan is thrown into the unfamiliar medical world of determining a course of treatment with varying options while trying to comprehend the medical terminology and significance of each option. Shannan so vividly explains the effects, the pain, and the indignities of chemo, radiation, and a bone marrow transplant in a way that we can almost feel what she experienced including the raw emotions that she confronted.

Through all that Shannan faced, she surrounded herself with close family members and close friends whose support sustained her through her cancer journey. These were the people who prayed, visited, brought meals, drove her to appointments, and contributed financially. We learn from her the value and importance of family and friends, who are present during the difficult periods of life.

The most astounding part of Shannan's story is her unflappable faith in God. We get a glimpse into her deep understanding of the Bible and how that is lived out during a period of personal crisis. She was consistent in prayer and praise to God throughout the highs and low of her journey refusing to lose her focus on Him. What a privilege to know such a woman of faith who has such an incredible story to tell.

Melvin Holder, Ed. D.

CHAPTER 1

The Disruption of Everything

⟋⟋ **Y**ou don't have pneumonia, you have cancer," the young, beautiful Grey's Anatomy-looking female doctor said in the most matter of fact way that I'm sure is exactly how she was taught to deliver such news. Just like that, those mind-blowing words turned my world upside down. My life experience already felt like I had been living with what felt like a constant wedgie that I was desperately trying to adjust. If I was one who cursed in my mind or under my breath like I used to do many years ago, this would be the perfect place to insert emphatic, explosive expletives. What do you do when you are minding your own business, living a somewhat mediocre, normal, decent life, pursuing professional and personal goals and just trying to get through each day, only to have your entire life experience disrupted by a cancer diagnosis? I wish I could say this is a rhetorical question so there's no need to respond. However, this book is meant to be an interactive "dialogue" with you, so when you see: ****ACTION ITEM**** I invite you to pause and imagine what you would think, feel and do if cancer disrupts life as you know it, i.e., your life or in the life of a loved one.

Cancer is like an unwanted, uninvited guest that shows up and makes itself known in ways that leave the resident annoyed, frustrated and angry. It doesn't ask for permission to take up residence, neither does it give fair warning (in most cases). It doesn't play fair but randomly picks and chooses who will be affected. It doesn't even care about age, gender, race, nationality, socio-economic background or privilege. Cancer brings with it so much dread that people don't even like to use the word, as though it is a dirty, disgusting curse word. A cancer diagnosis can happen to anyone at any time. That is a fact of life, especially in these times where several factors can lead to the revelation of this disease. Nobody wants to hear that they or their loved one has cancer, but sadly, it is a reality that many people must deal with.

My name is Shannan Lewis and I am a cancer conqueror, survivor and thriver. I am no expert on the subject of cancer, and I can't educate you on the various kinds of cancer. However, I will share my own experience along with the evidence that has been documented by medical personnel. According to the very popular WebMD website (2019),

> Cancer, also called malignancy, is an abnormal growth of cells. There are more than 100 types of cancer, including breast cancer, skin cancer, lung cancer, colon cancer, prostate cancer, and lymphoma. Symptoms vary depending on the type. Cancer treatment may include chemotherapy, radiation, and/or surgery.

I write from a place of personal knowledge because I have had the experience with lymphoma leukemia, and now I am on the other side of that diagnosis. It is this familiarity with the diagnosis, treatment and overall process that leads me to share with you, and everyone who could benefit in some way from what I observed, learned and experienced. Therefore, **this is thoughtfully, carefully and lovingly prepared for anyone who has been given a cancer diagnosis or has a loved one who is dealing with cancer. I want to help you prepare mentally, emotionally, spiritually and practically.** In addition, my hope is to share for the sake of others who will never experience this disease but want to know how to provide support to those who walk, will walk or have walked this journey. I am documenting my story (which I consider to be *our story*) for the many people who have asked that I write about my thoughts, feelings and the unfolding of events so they will get some semblance of what it was really like to deal with a cancer diagnosis and treatment.

Granted, I can only provide my own perspective based on experience. I can't speak on behalf of others who have maneuvered this challenge, therefore as you read/listen and interact, keep in mind that this is my reflection, my thoughts, my observation and no one else's (unless otherwise indicated). These are the kinds of things I wish that I had known when I started the cancer journey (or as I call it, "The 2017 Excitement"). As I share my story and the new perspectives I have formulated about cancer, I invite you to engage with the information by allowing me to take you on a journey through my words, Facebook posts, emails and YouTube videos. In order to really understand what I am sharing, I encourage you to read/listen to this book with:

- an **open mind** (as annoyed, unsure and worried as you may be feeling about cancer)
- a **decision** to engage by being interactive when prompted to do so (as noted by ****Action item****)
- a **willingness** to visit my YouTube channel entitled "Shannan Lewis' Conquering Cancer Journey"

- a **commitment** to apply whatever information you find useful

So, you or someone close to you has been diagnosed with cancer. Now what? You may be feeling inundated with information, speculation and trepidation. Your mind may feel like it's in a tornado that arrived without the courtesy of a warning. Anything and everything you're feeling is valid because it is possible that like me, you never asked for this nor saw it coming. People who are diagnosed with cancer automatically become members of an exclusive club that we never signed up for. It is for this reason that I believe the initial feelings, thoughts and reactions must be expressed. Don't allow anyone to tell you how to feel because it is not their body nor their journey. Feelings are valid because those are the ways we give voice to our emotions in order to process what is happening and all that is about to take place. People will try to tell you how to feel and believe me, they think they mean well. But this is YOUR diagnosis. Cancer hit your body or someone that is close to you, so you owe it to yourself to sit with the new information which will initially feel like an invasion and a disruption.

Be patient with yourself, grappling with this news (a.k.a. test results) will take time, especially if you had no symptoms or other indication that something was happening in your body. Some people take a long time to hear, accept and process this information in their minds which may lead others to think they are in disbelief and denial. Others, like myself, immediately go into survival fight mode by choosing to embrace the information in order to determine a plan of action. Either way is fine. Take the time you need to process the results so that you can embrace the fact that it is now a part of your life story. Pretending to do otherwise may delay the start of treatment and a plan of action.

I totally understand when someone doubts the diagnosis and goes into immediate rejection mode by thinking, "this isn't happening to me. Cancer affects other people, not me, not my family." People of faith sometimes take this approach. While this is a good thing based on the faith talk that says, "we believe the report of the Lord that by His stripes we are healed," choosing to stay in the place of doubt, disbelief and denial could delay the healing and recovery process.

ACTION ITEM

For more information, see
https://www.webmd.com/cancer/default.htm

CHAPTER 2

Life Before the Disruptive Diagnosis

I had a pretty decent life in 2016 even though it turned out to be filled with a few significant changes in my personal life. On the other hand, my professional life was thriving as the only admissions counselor and an adjunct professor at Palm Beach Atlantic University-Orlando. I gained great fulfillment in both my roles at the university, but nothing was more satisfying than my role as a mother to my Gifts from God, Shanel and Daniel (DJ). I took my mommy ministry very seriously by making sure that I was available and accessible both physically and emotionally. Add church involvement to the mix and this all made for a hectic life, but I thoroughly enjoyed the balancing act of juggling it all.

My coworkers and I were blessed with the gift of a free hotel stay that we could use whenever it was feasible, so I decided to get away mid-November 2016 without the children for the weekend. It was a long overdue mommy treat where I could unwind, process, pray, relax and reflect on the year that was ending in a few weeks. As indicated before, several changes and challenges had occurred that year, yet there I was still standing, still smiling, still committed to pursuing a path of emotional recovery, renewal, and rebirth. I was in good health, good spirits and "good to go" regarding my plans for the new year.

One of my professional highlights each year was attending the December graduation in West Palm Beach with a few of my fellow faculty members. The road trip always included singing, laughter, intense conversations and two hearty meals at a fine dining restaurant. Graduation represented the culmination of my students' accomplishments and a reminder that my roles as their admissions counselor and adjunct professor made a difference. In addition to the joys of being a mother, my occupation provided the most fulfillment and affirmation in my life.

Little did I know that in a matter of weeks my life was about to be disrupted, my students would be left without their assigned professor, my routines were going to be hi-jacked and my professional pursuits would be put on hold for an extended period of time.

CHAPTER 3

The Clues

When I was diagnosed with T-Cell Lymphoma Leukemia on January 10, 2017, I lay in that emergency room in shock. Given that I honestly did not see this diagnosis coming, total shock would be the expected response, but curiously and surprisingly, it wasn't. I had done all my annual physical and gynecological examinations in 2016 and all the results were excellent. I had a clean bill of health in every sense of the word. There was nothing happening nor symptoms indicating that cancer was in my body. However, looking back I had a few clues that I haven't shared publicly before now. I guess I am finally ready to admit that God was preparing me for the diagnosis even before it happened, but at the time, I was oblivious and dismissive. It is said that "hindsight is 20/20" so years later, as I am reflecting and recalling details from that time, I realize there were moments of foreshadowing that at the time I brushed aside. It's interesting to see how your memories will take you back to the months and even moments before the diagnosis in order to determine if there were clues that were ignored or minimized.

I have often shared that the first indication that something was wrong in my body happened the night of Friday December 16, 2016. **(In my Sophia Petrillo voice – the little old lady in The Golden Girls television show),** *Picture it, Friday night at The Christmas Hope Awards, Shannan looking stunning in a gorgeous black gown as she takes photos at the event and sings with the amazing choir at The River of Life Christian Center in Orlando, Florida.* The night was perfect in every way as my children and I strolled onto the red carpet, posed for our photos, and then went into the sanctuary to enjoy an amazing award ceremony for the church volunteers. In addition to enjoying the evening as an honored volunteer, I basked in two other favorite roles. I was invited to photograph the festivities alongside the other professional photographers, capturing several candid and posed shots around the venue, as well as several videos and photos during the award ceremony. Preserving life's moments in photo or video form is both a privilege and passion of mine. As a member of the choir, I was pleased to participate in the evening's opening song. It felt like being in a Broadway show as we excellently performed *Carol of the Bells* with choreography. I felt like a star; I felt like a Queen; I felt like it was going to be a great Christmas and that life would be good after all.

But something was different after the night's festivities ended. I felt a sore throat developing although at the time, I was grateful that it didn't happen before I sang exuberantly with the choir. When I arrived home, I knew my body had "picked up something" because it was giving me the signs of what could be a cold. Days later, I confirmed with my doctor that it was not a cold developing, but it was bronchitis. Needless to say, I had to take time off from work, cancel my front-line singing commitments at church and go on a mandatory vocal rest for the remainder of 2016. Not being able to interact with my coworkers or sing with my choir was a major disappointment. Little did I know that this was the beginning of a period of extended isolation and inactivity.

The 2016 Christmas season was upon us and although I was sick, I still participated as best as I could. The children and I enjoyed family moments, Christmas goodies and a wonderful visit from my best friend, Lorene Pinnock, and her family. My body was fighting bronchitis with the aid of antibiotics, but my spirit was as effervescent and excited as usual.

It was a year of challenges and changes, but the children and I made it through and were eager to see what 2017 was going to bring. The Prince and Princess were doing well in school and were involved in youth activities at our church. Life was far from perfect, but they seemed to be well adjusted and in good spirits. Mommy-Kids time at home meant preparing meals together, watching our favorite TV shows in my bed and having one-on-one candid conversations about anything they wanted to ask or talk about. I was very much aware of my mommy ministry and took it very seriously.

On a personal note, I was concerned about my weight gain and feeling tired frequently, so I decided to make a New Year's decision to make lifestyle changes. (I don't believe in New Year's resolutions because people often make, then break them.) I was not able to do much swimming that December because it was too chilly (plus I was dealing with the bronchitis), but I went to the gym with the children to get used to being on a treadmill again after years of not having a regular exercise routine. My plan was to utilize the gym at home and take 12 flights of stairs each day at work. These changes, along with adjusting my diet would certainly do the trick because I weighed about 175 lbs. and needed to bring that situation under control. (Hey, no judging allowed... you probably can relate to gaining weight and needing to bring it under control.) Anyway, that was the way 2016 ended for me. I had a plan in place to tackle my health, fitness and wellness.

Permit me to pause and probe (remember I indicated earlier that this is meant to be an interactive dialogue with you). So here goes.

ACTION ITEM

What Are You Currently Doing for Health, Fitness And Wellness?

Many times, we wait until a situation or sickness forces us to make the best decisions for our body, mind and spirit. Perhaps you are at a point in your life when it is time to have an honest conversation regarding your overall health and fitness. It does not mean you have to take things to the extreme, but it could mean that lifestyle adjustments may be needed to get you to a better place so that you can be healthier physically, emotionally and spiritually.

OK, let's get back to the unfolding of events...

On the night of New Year's Eve 2016, I prepared for the usual Watch Night church service to bring in the new year. I was particularly excited because we had a special guest from a well-known mega church ministering that night. Even though I was still sick with bronchitis, I worshiped and enjoyed the service as best as I could. I was feeling ready to conquer the new year and everything it was going to bring.

During one of the songs, the guest artist started doing an unplanned, unrehearsed, spontaneous victory chant. She made bold declarations encouraging the audience to respond with "I

WIN" each time she described a scenario that could occur in 2017. The crowd was on their feet and normally I would be too (I am a passionate praiser), but I was feeling tired because of the bronchitis and the late hour, so I stayed seated but chanted along with her and the audience. However, when she said, "Tell cancer I win", I became annoyed and triggered! I became upset and said nothing! I did not repeat that declaration because I did not want to associate the cancer word with my life. That was the **first clue** even though I did not know it then. It was almost as if something deep inside did not want to speak those words out loud and acknowledge the possibility that cancer could be in my future. I remained silent and became subdued. In the moment it struck me as odd, but a few weeks later, I asked a choir member to send me the video she recorded of the "I WIN" declarations. I knew it was a powerful prophetic moment, and although I paused while the crowd was chanting, I knew that I needed to play it repeatedly (even though at the time, my mind and my mouth did not participate). Looking back now, I recognize that this was a clue that my mind and spirit was trying to deliver, but at the time I dismissed it.

The **second clue** that I realized years later is that I had been feeling fatigue for several months but didn't really pay it any attention because I was living my normal life and working my usual schedule (university admissions counselor in the day and adjunct professor at night). I had recently changed my living arrangement and was doing very well adjusting to the new normal. It was stressful but not more than usual. The go-getter-take-the-initiative-and-give-life-everything part of me, was on a roll (active in church, busy on the job, being a mother to a teen and pre-teen, and basically juggling every ball that was being tossed to me in the juggling act called life). I was used to the emotional requirements needed to live an efficient life and there was no need to feel that fatigue would not be the result of those endeavors. I often told my university students to get used to feeling fatigued and tired all the time as they balanced being a full-time student, parent, employee, etc. So, I had that same attitude and approach to the constant feeling of fatigue that had become my norm. Frankly, it was typical for me to be in bed very early at night, so I thought that feeling tired all the time was simply my body getting older and single-handedly dealing with many life stressors. Furthermore, I had completed my usual annual physical check-ups (medical, labs and female related checks) and everything was fine. The results were all good, so I had no real reason to be overly concerned about feeling fatigue most of the time. As it turns out, frequent fatigue was a clue I missed, or perhaps dismissed.

Looking back now, I can admit that I certainly dismissed the **third clue** when my sister-friend-neighbor Zaneen Thompson took ill and was hospitalized during the latter part of 2016. When she was released from the hospital, the Lord whispered in my spiritual ear, "You're next. You're going to be in the hospital for a while, but you will be ok." Honestly, I didn't really pay that any mind or give it any thought. I simply tossed His words aside because I was not sick in any way, so I figured this was probably something that would happen much later in life and would probably be of no significance.

As I reflect on those three clues, I realize that my spirit, mind and body were sending me signals that something was going to happen to my health in 2017. But the most significant feeling that was a recurring thought/theme in the latter part of 2016 was an acute awareness that destiny and purpose were wooing me. I even told my close friends that I felt as though my time on the job was coming to an end and I didn't think it was because I was going to get fired or resign for another position. Somehow, I felt that something was going to happen that would connect me with a major part of my predestined purpose puzzle.

Consequently, when I was taken by ambulance to the emergency room on Tuesday, January 10, 2017, thinking that the bronchitis had possibly turned into pneumonia, I was not totally shocked when the doctor came back with the results of the blood work. While I did not expect to be given a cancer diagnosis, my inner gut had been given a few clues which had subconsciously lay dormant until reality hit. God used each of these as a form of foreshadowing and even though I minimized and dismissed each one, my spirit and mind were prepared when the diagnosis was delivered.

CHAPTER 4

Welcome 2017

I welcomed 2017 with enthusiasm, excitement and exuberance which led me to taking a few photos in my home on New Year's Day to seal the moment of expectation. I posed in my empty dining room believing in faith that at some point in the new year, I would be able to afford a decent dining table and chairs. Then I took more photos in my bedroom as a declaration that despite how life was unfolding, it was still a wonderful life.

As usual, my first Facebook post for the year was a bold and brazen declaration; a letter of sorts addressed to the new year.

Dear 2017,

You have finally arrived, and I am looking forward to the journey. God used the previous years to prepare and position me, so I welcome you with the confidence that I have in Him. Frankly, I could not live this life in my own strength or wisdom, but I don't need to because God's got me. At this age, I feel settled and secure in my own skin, comfortable and cozy in my own prefer-ences, eager and excited about what the future holds. I know you are coming with a mixed bag but that's ok because there is nothing you can bring that God cannot handle. I'm just along for the ride so He's in complete control. My goal remains the same—to be God's hands extended as I bloom where I am planted. Well, that's all for now, I simply wanted to say hello and give you fair warning that when you see, approach or interact with me, you've got to go through God first!!

Let's do this!! God and I are ready!!
Shannan

2017 certainly "heard" my bold and brazen declaration and came to test the truth of it all. I started the year embracing my belief that it's a wonderful life (I read those words every day because that wall plaque was beside my bed). Whenever we put certain things out in the atmosphere, we must be ready for those belief systems, affirmations and declarations to be challenged. Frankly, that fact was not lost on me in any way but honestly, I did not expect that it would have been challenged by a cancer diagnosis a few days later.

(*In my Sophia voice again*) Picture it, January 9, 2017, at Palm Beach Atlantic University-Orlando (PBAU). I was choosing to make it a new year of lifestyle changes by conquering six flights of stairs (12 in all if you factor in going up and coming down). I was not big on exercise so this commitment to taking the stairs everyday was my decision to take baby steps to get some amount of exercise. My body was feeling well enough to return to work in preparation for the Spring 2017 semester. As the only admissions counselor at the PBAU Orlando Campus, I was responsible for recruiting, interviewing, processing and accepting all students (undergraduate and graduate) each semester. In many ways, they were all my "babies", but it was even more impactful for me when

16

I shifted roles from being their admissions counselor to one of their first professors. That was where I think God did His best work through me at PBAU because I was able to use all my communication, counseling, cheerleading and coaching skills to help my students connect their career with their calling. Such was the feeling on Monday, January 9th, when my very close Jamaican sister-friend and fellow faculty member came to my office. Classes were about to begin but Andrea and I had not seen each other since the new year began. Furthermore, it had been a while since our last **Sisterhood Session.** Dr. Andrea Cunard and I share a special sister bond with Therapist Lisa Hoang and Pastor Sandra Valentine – the four of us have a bond of **SISTERHOOD** that is our safe, sacred space.

Our immediate embrace represented the usual sister friend salutation. Our hugs delivered support, strength and safety no matter what life was throwing at us. However, when we greeted each other that evening before we went to our classrooms, we had no idea it would be the last time in a long time that we would be able to share a hug.

There was no way to know in that moment that this was also the beginning of the end of my tenure as admissions counselor and adjunct professor at the university. We had no idea that cancer was going to invade our sacred space and prevent me from getting or giving hugs because my immune system was going to be compromised.

Let me pause briefly from the events leading up to the diagnosis to implore you to hug your loved ones regularly. Too many times we only hug those close to us if something bad has happened and we feel the need to comfort. Some only hug in a sexual context where it is shared as a part of the make out activities or as the foreplay routine for lovemaking. Yet giving and receiving hugs is such an important part of our life experience because it connects us with fellow human beings (not only those close to us). Looking back now, I am so grateful that Andrea and I shared this hug because it became very significant in the months that would follow.

When was the last time you hugged someone just for the purpose of showing love, acknowledgment, support and kindness? More importantly, do you hug the people who live in your home or is that reserved for the lovers who come and go, or friends and colleagues we give most of our time to? "According to scientists, the benefits of hugging go beyond that warm feeling you get when you hold someone in your arms...hugs reduce stress by showing your support..." (Cirino, 2018).

Back to the unfolding of events...

I taught my undergraduate Leadership students that Monday evening and felt excited about the new group that I was planning to impact through the curriculum, classroom conversations and our overall connection. Their academic journey began with me as their admissions counselor (from inquiry to acceptance in the program) and then as one of their first university professors. Class went well and I was tired but feeling expectant that this would be a great semester. However, life had other plans because when I arrived home that night, I felt extremely tired. When I woke up the following morning, the first thought that came to mind was, "I feel weird" (not tired, not sick, just weird). Anyway, I took a shower, had breakfast and drove to work.

As the morning progressed, I noticed that my heart was beating rapidly—I even brought it to my coworker's attention. One could look at my neck and see it throbbing. By this time, my breathing became labored, so my boss and co-worker suggested that I contact the doctor. I called my primary care physician and made an appointment for that afternoon. Being the "tough cookie" that I am, I tried to proceed with normal work activities, but my body decided to go into full rebellious mode. Out of an abundance of caution, I left work earlier than planned because it was obvious that I would not have been able to continue working until it was time for the afternoon doctor's appointment. I figured if I went home and rested before the appointment, I would feel better.

While driving home, I called the doctor's office to see if I could go in sooner than the early afternoon appointment, but their office was closed for lunch. By this time, I was driving in distress. I was struggling to breathe; my heart was beating rapidly and I was feeling weak. Something was definitely happening in my body and I became worried. Thankfully, I did not take the quickest route on the interstate (which would have gotten me home sooner) but instead, I drove the longer way which meant that I would have to pass my church on the way home. As I approached the building, I called the church office to see if I could go there instead of trying to drive myself home. I was relieved when my worship leader, LaRue Howard, answered the phone, and after describing what was happening to me, she said, "Come straight here."

As I drove into the church parking lot, my pastor's son and LaRue were waiting for me. Little did I know that that would be the last time I would be able to drive myself for a while. They immediately came to assist me and took me into the church lobby because I was feeling weak. By this time, I felt scared because my heart was beating like it was going to burst, my chest was tightening as though I was going to have a heart attack and my breathing was labored. My worship and arts director, Anthony Jenkins, checked my pulse using his Apple watch. His response was, "Your heart rate is just what mine would be like after leading a song on Sunday" (and if you know anything about the way we worship at The River of Life Christian Center, you know that we're passionate, powerful praisers). Something was wrong; something was happening. I was nervous and scared. The church administrator joined the four of us and asked if I wanted her to call 911 (this was protocol even though by that time we all knew that was the best decision that needed to be made). I immediately agreed because it was obvious at this point that I was not going to be able to keep that doctor's appointment. As we waited for the ambulance to arrive, the pastor's son took my car keys and LaRue took my phone so she could contact my family and coworkers. Once the ambulance arrived, LaRue took my bag and proceeded to accompany me to the hospital. And so, it began – the scary excitement, diving headfirst into the unknown, praying that it wouldn't be anything too serious.

Everything was happening so quickly that I didn't have time to give place to internal panic. As the emergency response team started asking questions and doing the necessary procedures, I could not think about anything other than my own self-diagnosis (you know how we tend to self-diagnose based on what we think is happening in our bodies). It felt surreal because I had never been transported in an ambulance before. The EMTs started working on me in the lobby of the church and continued in the ambulance. All this time I was thinking, "Oh shucks, this bronchitis is too ambitious. Why is this thing turning into pneumonia? I don't have time for this." (I am sure there was a Jamaican patois internal dialog going on, coupled with the heavy, exasperated, "I can't be bothered," sigh but I did all that in my mind). The caring EMTs treated me on the way to the hospital to assist with the tightening of the lungs so that I could breathe better. LaRue waited with me in the Emergency Room for hours and kept my family updated as I was given a variety of tests and a full lab workup.

Later that evening, my sister, Alecia Lewis (a.k.a. Allie), arrived from work and LaRue left. We made small talk and tried to make the best of this unexpected excitement. Both of us anticipated that after the results were reported, I would be treated and sent home, so we had good sister time trying to make light of the situation. But when the doctor arrived and in a professional matter of fact tone said, "You don't have pneumonia, you have cancer," (something to that effect, I can't recall the exact words verbatim) my sister and I responded with, "WHAT??!!!!"

The next words, sentences, questions, and movements happened in slow motion, as if someone set a DVR in rewind mode. I heard what each doctor who came in was asking and saying – *"Where are you from?" "Your white blood cells are through the roof." "Were you having any symptoms?"* They explained that this type of cancer is so rare that it is mainly found in the Caribbean and Japan. ("Well dang, I must be special," I remembered thinking with a somewhat sarcastic attitude.) The doctors proceeded to explain that normal white blood cell count in a healthy adult is between 4,000 and 11,000 – mine were overly ambitious as they were "swinging from the chandeliers" (my words). The white blood cells were dangerously in the very high thousands. After our discussion, it was determined that I was asymptomatic which meant that I had no symptoms that T-Cell Lymphoma Leukemia was present in my body. Apparently, it was always there but I had no symptoms until something (or a combination of things) triggered it and the cancer made its presence known (like an uninvited, unwanted guest). It was a good thing that I had bronchitis weeks before because if there had not been sickness that prompted this progression of events, it is possible that I would have continued living with no symptoms, only to have this disease suddenly destroy my life.

Let's go back to the very beginning of this "conversation" (you're reading or listening to this in the form of a book, but I am really having a candid conversation with you). As previously indicated, you may have been recently diagnosed with cancer or know someone who just got the "news". Now what do you do? After you go through the denial phase, after you sit with the reality of the diagnosis, after you get the preliminary details, after you cry your eyes out, after you get angry and cuss, after you question yourself about possible missed signs, after you feel like demanding immediate answers from God as to how He could allow this to happen, and after you decide who to tell and how much to share at the very beginning, what do you do?

First of all, depending on the nature of the diagnosis, you have to decide what your ***approach*** and ***attitude*** are going to be (emotionally, physically and spiritually). Ignoring the diagnosis isn't going to change anything and it is certainly not going to miraculously go away unless that is what God ordained for your life story. Therefore, it is imperative that you **make up your mind from the very beginning how you want to deal with this disruptive diagnosis**. Because let's call it what it is, or rather, what it feels like initially – the delivery of a cancer diagnosis is a disruption of everything. Now, I am not going to pretend or assume that I know what you are capable of as it pertains to making that kind of decision. Who wants to receive such news or hear of a loved one's cancer diagnosis, then respond by deciding what the appropriate attitude and approach should be? That seems absurd and utterly ridiculous! However, that is exactly what will be necessary to set the tone for this journey. By deciding on your preferred attitude towards the diagnosis, the patient and loved ones get to choose what their mental frame of mind will be going forward. Taking the time to choose an approach will also set things on a preferred path for dealing with this new situation. Whether it is decided to do nothing and live out one's days on one's own terms, or the choice is made to fight like hell by any means necessary, that decision provides the ***call to action*** where everyone (hopefully) gets on the same page and proceeds accordingly.

During those first hours and days after the delivery of the diagnosis, I decided that regardless of the process and the outcome, **I was going to be a VICTOR, not a VICTIM**. I had to make myself recognize that this was now a part of my life story and even though I did not ask for it, expect it or desire it, I certainly could not ignore or resist it. Others have chosen to hear a cancer diagnosis and immediately decide to become silent and secretive. In some cases, they withdraw from family and friends in order to protect them from having to deal with the reality of the diagnosis. Others choose to discreetly seek alternative/holistic treatment without sharing the information with loved ones and friends. As the one whose life is about to be completely turned upside down, you have the right to deal with the diagnosis on your own terms based on your personal beliefs, religious convictions (if any), core values, expectations and preferred way of engaging with people in your life. No one should berate or belittle you for being silent and private about the diagnosis if that is your choice. In the same token, don't allow anyone to put you down if you choose to be vocal and public about the diagnosis. People will always have something to say but it is your right to ignore comments and feedback if it goes against what you believe is best for you. **Choose the attitude and approach that best suits you and will serve others based on your preferred ways of engaging with your world**.

In my case, I did not have a choice to be silent or secretive about the cancer diagnosis because from the very beginning I realized that this was going to be an assignment that I had to fulfill. I knew that this was supposed to be an integral part of my life's journey. As I previously alluded to, the year before, I sensed that my life was going to change, and I was going to birth a significant part of my purpose and destiny. I even said to my close friends, "Destiny is calling me. I think that my time at PBAU is coming to an end." It was almost like I was pregnant with potential and purpose and knew that the delivery time was getting close. I knew from the moment of diagnosis that this was a necessary part of my life story and it would lead to the unfolding of other parts of my purpose and destiny.

When Allie and I heard the diagnosis in the emergency room, her response was, "No God! Daddy already took the hit for the family. He died from lymphoma at 42 years old. We're not doing this again." Our mutual shock was coupled with a feeling of injustice and unfairness. Our family already dealt with a cancer diagnosis which did not end with Daddy living. In fact, he was diagnosed at the beginning of 1990 and although treatment was given, he died in December of that same year. I understood my sister's reaction because it seemed like a cruel joke, but in the depths of my spirit, I sensed that if God allowed this to happen to us again, it meant He could trust me and my family to handle it well. Consequently, that belief framed my overall attitude and approach that I was going to submit to the cancer journey and make God proud, even if that meant I would also die because of lymphoma leukemia.

Later that night (diagnosis day), after I was admitted and transported from the Emergency Room to what would become my new room in the hospital, the reality of the situation began to sink in. I had a moment of "beating against God's chest'" like an angry child who felt that her parent was being unfair, unkind, unreasonable and unrealistic. As I prayed and questioned Father God about the diagnosis, reminding Him of all the other major life stressors that I was dealing with, He spoke very clearly to my spirit and explained why. *"**Shannan, I can trust you with this. You can handle it. Unlike many who choose to be silent, secretive and shut down when they get sick, you will share as you go***

through the process. You will help many people and My glory will be revealed through your journey. I have assigned people to go through this with you. This is not sickness unto death. Watch Me take care of you!" Father God's words comforted me and provided clarity that the sickness had purpose and was a part of His plan. This enabled me to shift from my pity party perception about the potentially painful process and put it in proper perspective so that I could be purposeful. The communicator and educator in me realized that I had to use my experience to educate and expose people to the real, raw realities of dealing with a cancer diagnosis. I also had to encourage and empower others through my transparency and candid communication so that people would be able to deal with their own situation. I knew beyond the shadow of a doubt that I had to become vulnerable and open about the process (even the ugly messy parts) in order to inform, inspire and impact lives. I had no idea what the journey would look like, but from the very beginning, I knew what I needed to do and how I was supposed to navigate this new terrain. I was scared yet submitted myself to the process as I embraced a winning attitude and approach.

As the days unfolded in my "temporary new home," I began sharing on Facebook and with loved ones. I knew that I could not keep silent about what was happening, so I shared whenever I felt prompted to do so. I instinctively knew that many would disapprove of my candid, transparent Facebook posts. I could almost hear the caustic, critical comments that certain people would make regarding my willingness to be vocal about parts of the cancer journey. Memories of criticism came to my mind, attempting to silence and prevent me from sharing honestly. I recalled things that were said years before which could have potentially placed me in a state of paralysis and would have prevented me from sharing as I needed to. But Father God silenced the caustic comments from critics by reminding me that He made me to be a communicator, an agent of positive change and an international, inspirational influencer. I was wired and designed to be an excellent communicator (written and verbal) who was blessed with an innate ability to convey what others felt and experienced in ways that appealed to the masses. I also remembered my pastor's popular saying, "Never allow the voice of a critic to be louder than the voice of your Creator" (Pastor Marvin Jackson). Consequently, whenever I wondered and even doubted if the Lord truly gave me this assignment to share openly about the cancer journey and other matters I deemed important, God ministered to my spirit with a reminder that He knew I would be able to convey what people were thinking, feeling and experiencing while connecting in ways that resonate with many. My mantra and mission became, "God will get all kinds of glory out of this," because I began to realize that as I submitted myself to the process and trusted God, the medical team, the prescribed treatment plan and my safe support system, many amazing things would happen during the journey. The delivery of a devastating diagnosis which could potentially disrupt every area of my life, was possibly going to bring disguised blessings for my good and God's glory. That was my attitude – that was my approach – that was how I chose to move forward into the unknown.

ACTION ITEM

See online article entitled "What Are the Benefits of Hugging?" written by Erica Cirino at https://www.healthline.com/health/hugging-benefits#1.

CHAPTER 5

Lifelong Preparation

Once I got my "marching orders" from the Lord and clarity as to how I should proceed, it enabled me to approach the diagnosis as a fight that I had been preparing for all my life and would definitely win. I realized that everything I had gone through in life prepared me for this battle that I was about to undertake. None of the experiences of my life were going to be wasted because they developed my emotional, mental and spiritual muscles. I had to summon solo strength, courageous GODfidence, and bravery to engage in this battle and win the fight. My mind went into a rewind setting as it did the rapid replay of several significant life experiences that trained me to bravely battle on my own.

I recalled the little girl (about 5 or 6 years old) being beaten, bullied and berated behind the church building by a group of girls who felt they needed to punish me for being sexually molested. They heard that I did "nastiness" with an older boy and took it upon themselves to punish me on behalf of my prominent public figure pastor parents. Weeks or months before, I was staying at a church member's home after school. The boy who was at the home said he was going to "_____" me as he led me to the room and had me lay on the bed. I had no idea what he meant or what he was going to do. I was a little girl who was still in kindergarten. I remembered the details as I was wearing my school uniform with crisp pleats in the skirt. In the moment, I was clueless as to what was happening as he penetrated my little body. I was too young to realize what had happened and seeing that he didn't physically hurt me, I didn't know that I was violated and that my innocence had been desecrated. It wasn't until I was taken to the back of the church during lunch time at Vacation Bible School, blamed and beaten by a group of girls, that I realized something bad had happened to me and that perhaps I was a "bad girl" as they kept saying. After that beating and taunting session at VBS, I remembered frequently going to the altar after my daddy preached so that I could get saved again, desperately trying to have my "sins" washed away each time an altar call was given, because some dumb bully told me that what happened was my fault and if my parents ever found out, they would kill me. I recalled the confusion, guilt and shame that I carried for years thinking that I was a "bad girl". It didn't help when others made inappropriate moves on me (in the church bathroom and in class at Primary School). I started thinking that maybe something was wrong with me, why people (male and female) liked to have their way with my little body. I wasn't even 8 years old, yet the little girl in me carried a burden so heavy that I was convinced I had to carry it all alone and in silence for many years. I remembered what it felt like to have to compartmentalize, internalize and minimize those feelings in order to smile, shine, excel in school, be actively involved in church events, and participate in family life all while trying to ensure that my parents would never find out. Thus began the struggle of solo fighting for self-preservation. I became used to dealing with difficult traumatic events on my own because I didn't know who was safe, sincere or solid.

I remembered the times as a child when I never felt good enough, pretty enough or smart enough, yet I had to push past those feelings because I was expected to be Pastor Lewis' perfect big daughter. It's amazing how church people, society and cultural expectations send subtle yet solid messages that a pastor's child should be flawless and always conduct themselves above reproach. One wasn't supposed to be less than a straight "A" student or be incompetent in social interactions. The pressure to be good and somewhat perfect was intense, but feeling like I had to overcompensate for the lie that I was a "bad girl" meant that anxiety and frustration became my closest companions. I was depressed most of the time but didn't really know that. I was often accused of being "moody", "fragile" and "sensitive", but the truth is I was fighting battles in my heart and mind that I couldn't share with anyone for several years.

I had the best parents in the world, an amazing family and a few loved ones, but I didn't want to trouble them with the things I was struggling with. In essence, I felt I needed to shield them from my internal battle, so I fought in silence, smiling, singing, and frequently speaking as a teen public speaker at retreats, graduations, on radio and television. I efficiently performed all the tasks and obligations that helped me silence the screams that were squashed on the inside. These feelings continued throughout my teenage years as I trained my mind to fight in silence, sadness and solitude, simply smiling, people pleasing and performing through the pain. I became an expert in going through difficulties and silently fighting on my own until I learned how to allow the Lord and the right people to help me with those battles. Thankfully through the years, especially in my teenage years, God sent the right people who helped me identify and address those areas of pain so that I didn't have to fight alone all the time.

I had years of preparation for life's tough fights not only because my entire childhood and youth was a battle of sorts, but because God saw fit to position me with spiritual people and in purpose-filled places so that through the years, I would receive a wide assortment of weapons for my arsenal. Once I began to discuss my childhood wounds, I could recognize and accept that the molestations were not my fault. I gained comfort, clarity and in some cases, closure as God provided the right avenues for healing. People were sent to pour into me even when I didn't realize that I was their assignment. As I grew into adulthood, career opportunities and ministry obligations provided access to resources that were meant to develop me personally, professionally and spiritually. Insightful leaders and mentors recognized the potential in my life and sought to teach me how to boldly become all that I was meant to be. In so doing, I began to develop a powerful place inside which I call the basement of my spirit. It is a deep well where I strategically and intentionally place my weapons – my arsenal – the things I use to combat negativity and difficulty. Through the years, as I got older, smarter and wiser, my well grew deeper with more substance, strength, stamina and strategies for living life effectively.

With time, tears, therapy and true love from God-approved people, I began to expand my emotional and spiritual well with the right weapons for life's battles. I learned the value of self-care (or as I now call it, self-sustenance). I reveled in the freedom of true worship that is life changing and totally liberating (not a few songs on a Sunday, but a lifestyle that brings change from the inside out). I boldly accessed the throne room of Heaven with audacious prayers and heartfelt daddy-daughter discussions. As I grew in my faith (through trial and error, mistakes and messy moments, falling and rising, forgiveness and grace), the contents of my well began to feel like a real reservoir filled with emotional and spiritual weapons that helped me navigate the challenges of life. Consequently, this was where I went in my mind and spirit whenever I found myself inching closer to the end of my rope in every situation, not just the cancer diagnosis. I could dig deep down on the inside and reach into this reservoir filled with significant life memories and experiences that provided persistence and resilience to handle the vicissitudes of life.

Days after the diagnosis, in the quiet alone moments, I climbed into that well and took a trip down memory lane. I went all the way back to the good parts of my childhood and teenage years. I realized that every family devotion with my parents and siblings, Sunday School class, church retreat, church convention, church youth camp, tent crusade, choir rehearsal and every time I ministered in song prepared me for the fight I was about to embark upon. I remembered how I lost my faith—no, not lost, I discarded my faith as they lowered my daddy's casket in the ground in December 1990. As I lay the Father's Day gift we had gotten for him that year on top of the casket, my faith in God went into the ground with him. I was still a practicing Christian, but I was cynical, critical and skeptical. I was annoyed that God didn't do what all the people said He would do. (Prayer warriors came and prayed very frequently, but a few told us that our daddy would be healed and would live.) Can you imagine what that kind of expectation does to children? Can you envision the confusion and chaos that was triggered when my daddy did not get better but died? I tossed my faith into that grave and lived with a "whatever will be, will be" mentality.

Thankfully, several years later, I regained my faith in God and became even bolder and more daring with it. I recalled the times I missed the mark and stumbled in my walk with the Lord, but

He cleaned and restored me every time. I reflected on the many battles I fought and won through the years by prayer, praise and practical application of learned life lessons. I vividly remembered that I had a proven track record with the Lord and that each one was like deposits that were made in my deep reservoir that I would now need to access in order to get through this season of sickness. I realized that all of these and many other things that occurred in my adult years prepared me for this fight and that I was going to win. People have often commented on my strength and have asked what gave me the courage and confidence to go through the cancer journey the way I did. My honest response is that it was daily doses of God's grace, the right support system and many years of preparation due to the various life challenges that I already went through.

Like Jesus' mother, Mary, who could not share these kinds of thoughts with others, I had to ponder all of this in my heart. My bold decision to go through this fight and win, was not something I could share like I felt it because to some, it would seem or sound like I was probably in denial and trying to minimize what was happening. I had to sit in it like a soiled diaper and be comfortable and confident enough to accept that no matter how this was going to progress, I had to embrace it all and do it well. My goal in the entire process was to make God proud and hope that in everything, He would get glory and lives would be inspired, changed for the good and helped in some significant way. As a Daddy's girl, I always endeavor to make God look good because He's kept His promise to be my Father after He took my earthly father when I was 17 years old. I really didn't have a choice but to accept and approach the diagnosis as more than a disruption; I had to be willing to consider the possibility that this could result in blessings in disguise.

Email Sent to My Choir & Church Leaders

On Feb 23, 2017, at 8:17 AM, Shannan wrote:

My River Family,

I miss you all so much but I am grateful for your service at The River of Life. I am so proud to be a River member and honored to serve with you all. Although I understand why I have to be away for a while, I hate being away from my choir, my church, my River leaders and family. It is hard to feel stuck and unable to be around people but I am submitting to the process and trusting God with the purpose. My desire is that He gets all kinds of glory from my life and especially this unexpected situation.

My reason for writing is to ask that you not take your membership at The River for granted. Being involved in a church that is vibrant, life giving and transforming is a blessing. So many ministries in Orlando lack what we have at The River (a spirit of excellence, a sound organizational structure, leaders who care and keep it real, a team of volunteers who are equipped to serve effectively, money to fund the vision, great music, an anointed worship team, relevant Word and so much more). DO NOT TAKE ANY OF THIS FOR GRANTED. Always appreciate the leaders, each other, the various gifts and opportunities available at The River of Life.

I know that it is normal to get weary in well-doing and feel drained with the weekly obligations and requirements (rehearsals, planning meetings, two or three services, etc.). But I implore you to rest when needed, but come back stronger and better. One of the hardest parts of this sick season is that I am not able to attend choir rehearsals (those Thursday rehearsals were life giving), sing each Sunday, worship freely and leave service feeling fueled. I don't like having to rely on Live stream or people's Facebook videos to experience what is happening at The River. I HATE

THIS!!!!! I hate not being able to hug on you all and be loved by you all. I miss hearing Shondell's prayers before we sing. I miss the Ricola candy and the sound checks. I miss having a free worship experience as I break my alabaster box each week. But this is the path God has permitted so while I hate it, I appreciate what He is doing and trust Him to get me through to total healing. PLEASE TAKE YOUR SERVICE AT THE RIVER TO THE NEXT LEVEL. Make the necessary personal adjustments to facilitate being able to be on your post when required. It is easy to blow this off or say, "others will be there", but we (sick or those who can't attend) need you to be there (present and accounted for, on your post, in position). Even if you feel tired, please tap into the anointing and give everything (especially if the cameras are rolling). The live stream audience only gets to see and experience your energy so we need you to go all the way in from the moment you hit that stage. Slip out of self and give way to the Holy Spirit so He can use each of you (even if you are on the back row). Those cameras capture almost everything, so always keep your praise, facial expressions and body language on point. Forget being cute or looking camera-gorgeous. Give everything because I need what you have, the congregation needs you to help pull them up to that next level and the live stream audience relies on you to usher us in.

I know this is for the choir but it could apply to any area of the ministry. We never know which service could be our last (and I mean that because I don't know when I will be able to sit in a service again or if the Lord is going to use this sickness to usher me Home). Therefore, I encourage you all to see your service at The River through different eyes and with a new sense of urgency and loyalty. Serve, sing and do all for the Lord, not for people, not to please or impress, not to position yourself for a better position, but for the Lord Jesus. That is our reasonable service. I am relying on each of you, God is depending on you too.

Thanks for your prayers, kind wishes and support. God bless you all–see you sooner than later (I am waiting for my miracle).

Love and hugs,
SHANNAN

Facebook Post:

Jun 27, 2017, 8:42 PM

I give thanks tonight for my River Worship Leaders, LaRue Howard and Anthony Jenkins. It's bedtime for patients but I hear these two in my ears—rehearsal techniques, anointed singing, encouraging words, cheerleaders. So all I can do is relive the memories as I worship on this bed and envision my return. I have learned so many great songs from them that at night, there is a playlist in my head. Grateful to be led by passionate praisers, prayer partners and warring worshipers.

CHAPTER 6

Preparing For the Possibility of Death

N ow, don't think for one minute that I was in denial about this devastating diagnosis. One of my doctors described it to my family this way, "We are dealing with two tigers, not a little cat" (referring to lymphoma and leukemia). The medical team did an excellent job explaining about the rare form of cancer that I had. The professor in me listened to the information as though I was grading an oral presentation or an APA research paper, paying close attention to the pertinent points. However, it was so overwhelming that I am grateful to have had my mother, Joyce Wallace, with me to take notes and keep track of everything. It is very important that you have someone who can be composed, attentive, observant and intelligent enough to ask the right questions, take accurate, detailed notes and advocate for you. If you are the patient, be forewarned that your body and mind will not be able to process at the same mental capacity once the sickness begins to take its toll and treatment starts to exhibit the effects.

Chemo brain is a real thing, so choose the right person(s) to document and keep detailed information on your behalf.

Armed with all the relevant information about what I was dealing with, I had to consider the possibility of death and wrestle with those thoughts as I would any other challenging life situation. I had to do it alone – no one could do that part for me (but as I previously indicated, life had trained me to take on these kinds of tough battles on my own). I had to venture down into the basement of my spirit. I had to walk along the deep corridors of my mind, go into the corners of my heart and reach out towards the crevices of my soul to make peace with the possibility that an untimely death could be the outcome. **Life does not teach us to deal with our own mortality because we spend so much time making a life that we rarely prepare for the eventual and inevitable end of that life.**

****ACTION ITEM****

Permit me to ask you these questions and I encourage you to pause, ponder, then answer honestly. I also suggest that you write your answers somewhere so that your loved ones will be able to retrieve them as a reminder if/when "life", I mean, death happens.

Questions to help you evaluate how well you are preparing for the end of your life.

1. *What are you doing now to prepare for the end of your life?*
2. *What kind of daily decisions are you making to ensure that when it is time for you to die, you would have lived well?*

3. **What would people honestly say and think about you when they hear of your death?**
4. **What will be your legacy?**
5. **What do you need to change now in order to live the kind of life you want to?**
6. **What kind of insurance do you currently have in place?**
7. **Who would you want to take care of your children if you are an adult with young kids?**
8. **Who knows where to find your will? Do you have an updated will?**
9. **What are your preferred end of life wishes and preferences?**
10. **What is your current relationship status with your Creator?**

Processing and facing the possibility of my own mortality allowed me to realize three important matters that I admitted and articulated to myself:

1) *I didn't want to die at an early age from cancer because it didn't have authorization to take me out as I wasn't finished living yet.*
2) *My decision and determination not to die was also for my children, my family and friends because I wanted to protect them from the devastation of premature death.*
3) *I was not afraid of death because it meant I would go Home to Heaven (and not because that's what people think automatically happens, but because I had accepted Jesus Christ into my heart and was living a consistent, consecrated Christian life).*

That being stated, (brace yourself if you think you knew me very well at the time I was diagnosed because this next part may come as a shock to you)—if God had chosen to take my life during 2017, I would have accepted it as His way of ending what was a disappointing life experience at that time. (***Exhale and expel a long, loud sigh.***) I have had a challenging life and even though it was also good in many ways, when this diagnosis came, I would have been ok with dying because life at that point in time had not turned out the way I expected. (**Don't get this part twisted or confused – I DID NOT WANT TO DIE; I WAS NOT WISHING FOR DEATH; I WOULD NOT HAVE EVEN CONSIDERED SUICIDE AT THAT POINT IN TIME**). I rested in and resolved within myself the possibility and realization that if death was the way God intended for my story to end in 2017, I would have accepted it. I had to make peace with the possibility that perhaps I was going to have a short life story. Don't misinterpret or misunderstand in any way. I was not accepting death due to cancer, but at the time, I would not have been totally devastated if that was the outcome shortly thereafter. I am sure that this may be hard for my loved ones to read, but each time I have deleted this sentence, I realize that in 2017, that was my truth. It's the messy truth that I wasn't going to accept death because I wanted to live, but in the same token, I accepted the possibility that if I died that year, I would be ok because I would end the sadness of a life filled with many disap-pointments (not anger, not rage, not sadness, not depression, but a lot of disappointments piled up through many years).

This admission just shocked many people because the Shannan they know is an exuberant, energetic, excited woman who exudes optimism, hope, inspiration and faith. THAT IS SO TRUE – THAT IS WHO I AM AT THE CORE, but that is not the total truth about how I was feeling at the end of 2016 and the begin-ning of 2017. Life had dragged me through the wringer, and I was worn out, whipped and emotionally exhausted. I did the best I could with what I had to work with. I responded and reacted from places that were hurt and unhealed for years. I kept trying to hold it all together to maintain the appropriate image, but my heart could only carry so much and no more. Life had turned out to be a mixed bag that doled out more difficulties than delights.

"Why Shannan, what do you mean?" you may be asking/wondering. Here's the thing, I had a decent life for the most part, but it was also filled with disappointment about many things. When 2017 arrived, I wasn't angry, sad or depressed about my life; I just felt disappointed about the way it unfolded. Don't get me wrong, it wasn't all bad – no one has a perfect life; I had my share of good, bad, and everything in between. That's life!! However, at that point in my journey **it had all taken a toll (all of it). I wasn't depressed or discouraged but I felt downtrodden**. My life felt like it had been a constant struggle from childhood. The life experience that I had up to that point left me feeling emotionally drained, depleted, disheartened and disillusioned. I was constantly having to fight for some semblance of peace, a sliver of the American dream and some amount of joy. I smiled most of the time, but not because I was happy (what the heck was that???). I hadn't really known what it felt like to be truly happy in a very long time. I smiled most of the time because I trained myself to greet the world with the gift of a smile (even if it was fake sometimes). I perfected the art of smiling because I had to be strong in public, because I cried a lot by myself in private. I had to be stoic, as if certain things didn't really matter or hurt. I had to silently stand even when everything seemed like I should fall apart. Thus, when cancer manifested itself, it joined many areas of my life that were already bruised, bleeding and broken. I was weary, worn out, worried and wounded. I was alive for many years but was not really living.

POEM: THE LIVING DEAD
written by Shannan Lewis many years ago

Living in a cemetery
Buried but not dead
Feelings and emotions
Cluttering my head
Lots of disappointments
Frustration and despair
Painful, hurting memories
I seem to hold so dear
Loads of bitterness and anger
Searching for a voice
Needing some expression
Wanting another choice
Existing issues unresolved
Threatens to overwhelm
Masks and facades melting
Peeling by themselves
Smiles no longer radiate
Sadness coming through
Laughter sounds like mockery
The truth is in clear view
Yearning for an expression
A replacement for numb
Needing a change of some kind
Can't stand being so glum

Life wasn't all bad though, because although that was my reality at the time, God had started me on a path of self-discovery, emotional excavation and healthy healing, but I wasn't whole yet. Although I was in the process of healing those parts of myself, there was so much more to be done. Healing included counseling and having a small, safe Sisterhood where I could share any- and everything. Healing emerged as I forgave and released people whose presence and participation in parts of the stage play of my life left places of bitterness. Healing came through times of brokenness in a church where no one knew me as I could sit in silence and allow God's words, the worship and the warmth of people to envelop me. Healing came as I surrendered to the sounds of nature (which I didn't realize was therapeutic to my entire being). The sound of waterfalls and thunderstorms became integral to my body's ability to relax in these gifts of nature. Healing came as I evaluated every part of my life and accepted that it all unfolded according to the Divine Plan of God. I allowed myself to see my life like a theatrical play where God wrote the script and determined the main characters, the extras, the conflicts, the setting, the scenes, and the switches that were necessary to bring the story of my life to the "stage". Yes, healing had begun to manifest, especially in 2016, but it was not yet complete. Consequently, I had to consider that death could have been God's chosen way to bring the curtain down on the stage play of my life. Years later as I write this, I am glad He didn't decide to end my life at that time and in that way. I have so much more to do, be, see and say.

Although I was hoping for the best outcome, I also had to consider and plan for the worst if that was going to happen. It started with imagining what death would be like. I envisioned dying peacefully in my sleep as Father God welcomed me with words like, "Shannan, you did well my daughter. You fought a good fight; you finished your course and you kept the faith." I imagined what it could be like when I arrived in Heaven.

(*In my Sophia voice again*) *Picture it, Shannan settles in for the night, relaxed and carefree, singing and worshiping as she sleeps. At the predeter-mined time, the assigned angel arrives to deliver her promotion papers. He gently nudges her in her sleep as he whispers, "Shan, it's time to go Home. Your time on earth is over." Shannan hears him as she changes position still fast asleep in the fetal position. Her lips curl in a smile one last time as the life-giving breath leaves her body. In that instant, her heavenly escort transports her from time to eternity. One moment she's sleeping like a baby and the next moment she struts daintily and victoriously onto the streets of gold. The light and love surround her so warmly that she is not able to wrap her mind around the significance of what just happened because she is too overcome by the magnificence of the moment. In the not too far distance, she hears the unmistakable voice of her father, Eric Lewis, shouting to a large group of sup-porters and cheerleaders, "Shannan is here; my firstborn made it Home!! Despite everything she had to go through all her life, she made it Home."*

Thus begins the reunions as I am greeted with hugs and con-gratulations. Being in my daddy's arms again made living worth it all. I spent my entire life trying to live so that I could have this moment again. I am greeted by my grandparents, my godmother and many others who were always cheering me on while I lived. But nothing prepared me for my first meeting with God the Father, God the Son and God the Holy Spirit. After what seems like hours worshiping in His presence, God assures me that He knew I had a long list of questions and things that needed to be clarified about life. Everything about life made sense and it was all worthwhile because I made it Home. (End of Heaven Imagination).

Now take a deep breath, dry your tears if you were crying and relax – that was just the way I envisioned it would happen. But I don't have any plans to die anytime soon. I fully expect to live a good, long life in the land of the living. Now keep on reading...

As exciting as being in Heaven was in my mind, my heart and my spirit knew it wasn't my time yet. My assignments were not finished and the life I have always envisioned hadn't even happened yet. I was in my early 40s, but had not really lived a good life yet (nothing remotely close to the life I expected and hope to live). The awesome, amazing, abundant life hadn't arrived yet. I was not yet in the position financially to do the things I wanted to do and give my children the life I always wanted them to have. I hadn't had a chance to spoil and pamper my mom like I always wanted to. I had not traveled to anywhere that felt truly spectacular. I had not experienced real tourist type vacations. I only went on one cruise for a few days many years ago. I did not know what it was like to enjoy the finer things in life, the kinds of things most people take for granted. Furthermore, I still had many lives to reach, so much more to learn, and many lessons to apply in order to determine if I would get them right. I was still in the process of evolving into the person God designed when He created me. I was still full of audacious aspirations and bold, unrealized dreams. I was bursting with a deep, robust, mature love that I needed to share. I was carrying around grand goals and inspirational ideas. I was pregnant with potential, plans, possibilities and purpose. **I could not die because I hadn't really lived yet. I could not die because I was too full and was nowhere close to being empty**.

Additionally, my biggest concern about dying was the loss that my children would experience. I did not want my kids to lose their mom at a young age like my siblings and I lost our dad as young teens. I took (and still take) my role as a mother very seriously. Cancer was not going to rob me of my God-given assignment in my children's lives, especially in the teenage years. My mommy ministry in their lives was not finished so I wasn't ready to die yet. In many ways Shanel and Daniel were my biggest motivation to live life well.

I was also concerned for my mom, siblings, and close relatives. Having lost Daddy to lymphoma, I did not want them to go down that path again. Many things changed after Daddy's death and I did not want them to suffer that kind of loss. I was also worried for my dearest, sincerest friends (I am blessed to have several special significant people – social butterfly that I am) but I am closely connected with very few. My death would have been devastating and I did not want that to happen to any of my family or friends.

The planner and organizer in me still did my due diligence, as I took the time to sort through important documents, update my will, write my end of life wishes and provide specific directions for the celebration party in case God did not grant my desire and took me Home sooner rather than later. I sent it to a few special people so that Mommy and my siblings would not have to worry about planning that event if it happened. In addition, I reminded my family that if I died, no funeral service was allowed. I don't like funerals at all!!! I get it, I understand that it is an integral part of our cultural norms as it pertains to honoring the dead, paying our last respects and supporting the bereaved family. However, I have always taken issue with all of that because funerals are really designed for the ones who remain and that was not my desire for my loved ones.

After my dad died, I looked at funerals very differently. I knew that I would never want one. I did not like the tradition of honoring the dead in that manner because, by the time someone was deceased, it was too late to honor and show respect. Instead, I wanted a celebration party—no flowers, no dark colors, no church service, no sermon. I wanted to celebrate my life BEFORE I died. My friends were given instructions that if I deteriorated to the point where it became obvious that death was inevitable, I wanted the party before I was promoted to Heaven so that I could hear the words, see the laughter, join in the tears, share the jokes, sing, dance, and share the gift of presence so that I could go Home with those meaningful memories. I didn't want the extravagance of a funeral service – no casket, no hearse, none of the traditional ways we honor the dead. I wanted to be cremated and have my ashes scattered in a body of water (no big fuss, just support and love for my children and loved ones). Life has taught me that it must be lived and celebrated while we have it. Death is too late to tell people, "I love you, I'm sorry, I was wrong, I appreciate you, I was impacted by you, I admire you, I was blessed and became better because of you."

****ACTION ITEM****

Stop reading for a moment so you can do one or more things you know you need to do now, or put plans in place to do them soon, while you have life.

What do YOU need to do?

> *Make the phone call that you have been putting off.*

> *Apologize to the person who needs to hear you say, "I am sorry" and mean it.*

Tell the significant people what they mean to you and don't assume that they already know.

Write a letter to the people who made a big difference in your life.

Email your boss, coworkers and colleagues to express appreciation.

Call your church office and express appreciation for the pastor and administrative team.

Forgive yourself for what you did when you did not know any better.

Hug your spouse for more than a few seconds (with no sexual favors expected).

Commend your children with words that carry great weight.

Write notes of thanks, affirmation, and encouragement and hide them in various places.

Stop taking the people in your life and phone contacts for granted.

Here is an example from a portion of my End of Life Wishes which were sent to a few key persons (make it your own; express what is most important to you):

Shannan's Parting Wishes (My Say, My Request, My Desires)

If the Lord chooses to promote me during this season of sickness (not later when I am old and have done all the amazing things I want to do), please adhere to and honor my current wishes being made here on March 20, 2017, at 4:20 a.m. from my 10933 Florida Hospital bed (good spirits, clarity of thought and accepting of God's purposes regardless of what they will be).

- The children and family should not see me dead unless they insist for closure or a last touch.

- Cremation should be soon after with my remains scattered by the lake at PBA or the pond at Oasis. If those places won't work, find a body of water and let it loose. Water was always my sacred, soothing element.

- The official celebration should not take place weeks later – the sooner the better.

- River of Life would be my preferred church or another really festive party type place. Truth be told, I don't necessarily want a church to be my last place of public celebration though – nothing churchy at all – just celebration, worship, singing, dancing, reflections, jokes, inspiration, music, laughter.

- If a church is used, then the officiating ministers should be Pastor Marvin Jackson and Pastor Leslie Pinnock. The female ministers should be Bishop Joyce Bernard, Pastor SR and Apostle Sandra Valentine (three female ministers who have had the greatest impact on my life spiritually and emotionally).

- I do not want a casket, an urn or flowers. The only visual representations should be photos of me and the people that matter doing the things I loved (being with my kids, family, students, public speaking, worshipping, singing, etc.). Show the things I did through photos. The other visuals should be the words I spoke especially in social media. That became a platform of purpose that was used to touch lives. Show my words and my face. Show that my short life mattered!!!

- Regardless of the location, I don't want it to be a church service type of celebration. I want it to feel like a production with worship and arts elements. No preaching allowed, just good inspiration and celebration. Praise, worship, dance, mime, Spoken Word, etc. A real production that takes people on a journey and makes them want to live life with more passion and purpose for the Lord and each other. Anthony Jenkins at the River and my Nucleus Creative Arts Team could help with this. Lorene Pinnock could also work with coordinating what this would be like.

- Dress should be comfortable, not formal. My SISTERHOOD should be identified by coordinated colors (preferably red and white with pearls – red is my favorite power color).

- Ideally this should not be a long drawn out event that will require feeding people afterwards. I so detest the idea of having the grieving family cater a feast for those who attend. If it is financially feasible, light food and beverages could be served after. However, it should not be so long that people get growling tummies.

- Allie and Otty don't need to do anything unless they want to perform or speak. I want them to be ministered to and loved upon. However, if they do, they need to turn up and bring a show that makes me dance in Heaven.

- River of Life choir could do an opening worship song but if not, that could be done by a praise dancer (Rachel Clark–Steph comes to mind because of her pure passionate dancing).

- Shanel and DJ don't need to do anything unless they want to perform or speak. Same thing with Mommy. It is more important for me that they feel no pressure to perform or do anything they don't want to do. They must be loved on and ministered to.

- There must be some representation from PBA – that could be reflections from students, faculty or staff but my PBA family must have a voice because that was my other home and safe place for many years.

- At some time, there must be an opportunity for personal reflection and re-dedication to the Lord as it pertains to living a life of purpose and intention. Cards should be provided for people to pause and write (that is the Professor part that would ask them to write down what they need to do now in order to live a better life no matter how much time they have left). This would not be like an altar call but a call to action for everyone to look within, write it down then see how they can live better, be kinder, make amends, choose a higher way of living that pleases God and cares for others.

- No releasing of doves or weird music at the end. High praise and prayers should signal the end of the celebration and music should be played as people exit.

- A commitment book should be in place for people to pledge their support for my family by providing their names and contact information so that when the realities of the loss and return to life kicks in, there is a list of people who have made themselves available to pray, call, connect, help, be there, etc. In addition, it would be like a guest book so that years from now, my family can look back and see who attended and still stayed in their lives.

That's it for now...the only other request would be this: if things get to the point where my days are numbered and we have time, I would like to do this in a smaller, more intimate setting with key people, and do a final celebration where I can actually hear people share and be able to respond. It would be my way of attending my own homegoing before I actually leave. It would not need to be morbid, but special and meaningful. OK, that's that... just want to be realistic in case God's timeline for all this is shorter than we want (like 2017/2018 type of departure). I strongly doubt that is His plan but still want to make sure you are all aware of my current wishes (just in case). Love you all!!!!

Shannan

CHAPTER 7

Embracing the Process

I begged God several times for a swift, supernatural miracle. I pleaded and negotiated that I would be a great demonstration of a contemporary healing – a real-life walking, living miracle. "Take the win," I would yell in frustration as if He didn't see that this could be His opportunity to show off through me and marvel many in the medical field. Obviously, God didn't take the bait by granting my heart's desire for a supernatural, spontaneous miracle that defied my medical team. Instead, He told me to go through the process so that I could inform, inspire and influence many lives. His unwillingness to "let this cup pass from me" (like Jesus had requested in the Garden of Gethsemane) provided many opportunities to live out my life's philosophy, "Bloom where you're planted."

I adapted that attitude and approach to life a few months after I turned 17 years old. Daddy's cancer had returned in the latter part of 1990 after seeking treatment in the United States for most of that year. He told Mommy that he wanted to return to Jamaica to be with his family instead of going through the process again. One Sunday, I stayed home with him because he was too weak to attend church or be out in public. As I listened to a sermon on the radio, I heard the preacher say the words, "Bloom where you're planted," and somehow it resonated in my spirit and became the theme and direction for my life. Little did I know that weeks later, I was going to put this theme in motion the night Daddy died. As I lay in bed that night, just as I was dozing off to sleep, I "saw" Daddy laying in a casket wearing his black and red clergy robe. Immediately, I knew in my spirit that he was gone. In that same moment, the phone rang, Mommy answered, then let out a blood curdling scream. I leaped out of my bed, ran to her room, took the phone and received the news that Daddy had just transitioned to his Heavenly Home. In that moment, I had to make a choice—I chose to bloom as I thanked the nurse (or whoever the lady was who had called from the hospital), then proceeded to call the key persons who needed that information. Although I was holding the phone while standing in what felt like a muddy, disgusting place that early morning (it was about 2 a.m.), I made myself bloom where I was planted as the peace and composure of God took over my mind and words. The next morning, my young cousin and I took the bus to register the death. I couldn't allow myself to feel the grief or mourn at that time because I had to be the big girl and bloom where I was planted. Thus, when cancer arrived in my own life 25 years later, I resigned myself to living out this philosophy seeing that God was obviously not going to snap His fingers, speak a word and give me an instantaneous healing. I had to humble myself and embrace the process so that I would not abort whatever purpose was wrapped up in the cancer journey.

An integral part of embracing the process was the realization that having **insurance,** a **solid support system** and the appropriate **treatment plans** were going to be a huge part of the experience. If you are about to embark on or are already going through your cancer journey, or perhaps you know someone close to you who is currently embarking on their cancer process, please consider each of these important matters which will help to make a big difference.

Insurance

Whether you have just started dealing with the health challenge or have been doing this for a while now, you are familiar with the check-in procedures at all medical facilities. Being able to present proof of insurance is a critical part of the process. Having gone through this experience allowed me to see the importance of having good medical insurance and life insurance. It also gave me compassion and sympathy for those who are not able to afford decent health coverage through their employer's group plan or private insurance.

Thankfully, when I was diagnosed, I was covered under my employer's group health insurance, which turned out to be excellent coverage. It made me appreciate the times I took home less money in my paycheck in order to get the benefits for me and my children. However, I realized while going through my health challenge and sharing with others, that this is not the case for many people. Health insurance is so costly in the United States of America that most are not able to afford the kind of quality coverage that is needed. Other cancer patients and people close to my heart shared their personal horror stories of how they lost their usual standard of living (home, vehicle, ability to pay bills, etc.) because of the medical expenses and lack of insurance coverage. I could share my thoughts on the matter from a political and social perspective, but I refrain from doing so because that is not my purpose for sharing in this medium. However, I do understand the plight of those who suffer because of the way healthcare and insurance coverage is handled in America.

The message that I want to convey is that one must carefully choose health insurance (and disability coverage) based on needs and not just cost. If you are fortunate to be employed with health insurance coverage as a part of your benefits package, ask probing questions and do research before the benefits enrollment is conducted. Read all the pertinent details and fine print provided in insurance packages so that you will know what is covered, deductible amounts, copayment amounts and all the other important matters that could impact your life if sickness occurs and you are not financially prepared. If possible, begin saving not for the "rainy day" but for unexpected health challenges. The cost for ambulance transportation is extremely high. Being able to pay the required deductible can also be costly if you have not set aside funds to do so. Sadly, this is the situation that many people find themselves in, because there isn't enough money to cover all the needs in a month. Regardless of your current financial situation, I implore you to make an emergency fund a matter of priority. Make the necessary lifestyle changes that will allow you the ability to save consistently to ensure that funds are in place when sickness occurs.

I am fully aware that for many people it becomes a matter of choosing a healthcare plan that will provide adequate insurance coverage and still be able to take home a decent paycheck. That was my own experience because I carried the insurance for the family for most of my life. However, I implore you to treat this matter with great importance because the alternative is difficult to deal with when you already have a health challenge to face.

If you are unable to receive insurance through an employer's group plan, take advantage of private insurance to ensure that you have coverage. Do research to gauge the benefits and limitations of purchased private insurance vs. government pro-grams. Do not make assumptions or listen to people's stories because everyone's situation is different. Ask pertinent questions regarding eligibility, cost sharing, out of pocket costs, etc. Take the time to evaluate your needs and those of your family so that the best plan can be selected. The time to have these questions answered is not when you are being admitted in the hospital. It is best to know these things ahead of time if sickness decides to pay you a visit and disrupt your life.

In the same token, buy life insurance so that your loved ones will be taken care of in the event of your passing. Certain cultures minimize the need for life insurance because they do not recognize the value but mostly, they don't acknowledge that death is inevitable. In a blog entitled, **"Six Reasons People Don't Buy Life Insurance (And Why They're Wrong)"** , Helen Mosher (2017) indicates that "most people put off buying life insurance" because they think that:

1. *It's too expensive*
2. *It's for babies and old people*
3. *They are strong and healthy*
4. *They have life insurance through the job*
5. *They don't have kids*
6. *They plan to get it eventually*

The reality of life is that none of us are going to get out of life ALIVE (unless you are still living when the good Lord comes back). That being the harsh reality, it means there will be loved ones left behind who may be financially impacted after you are gone. In the words of Helen Mosher, "don't let your *'eventually'* turn into your loved ones' *'if only'."* Once again, I implore you to do the necessary research to determine the most suitable type of life insurance that you need to obtain. According to explanations retrieved on trustedchoice.com:

> *The dollars you pay into **term life insurance** premiums are only there to provide a death benefit to your beneficiaries if you die during a specified **term**, while money you invest in **whole life insurance** premiums builds cash value that you can use later in **life** or that will add to the death benefit payout. (Huneck, 2020)*

The article also provides the following features of term life vs. whole life insurance:

Features of Term Life Insurance.

- Provides death benefits only
- Pays benefits only if you die while the term of the policy is in effect
- Easiest and most affordable life insurance to buy
- Purchased for a specific time period, such as 5, 10, 15, or 30 years, known as a "term"
- Becomes more expensive as you age, especially after age 50
- The term must be renewed if you want coverage to be extended beyond the term length
- Can be used as temporary additional coverage with a permanent life insurance policy
- Can be converted to whole life insurance

Features of Whole Life Insurance.

- Covers you for life
- Provides death benefits as well as a cash value accumulation that builds during the life of the policy
- You typically must qualify with a health examination
- Can be purchased without a medical exam, but at a higher cost
- Takes 12 to 15 years to build up a decent cash value
- Can be a good choice for estate planning
- Cash value is based on how much the return on investment is worth
- A portion of the cash value can be withdrawn or borrowed during the life of the policy
- Initially has more expensive premiums than term life insurance, but can potentially save you money over the life of the policy if in force for a considerable number of years

An essential part of embracing the process and preparing for the journey (short term and after recovery), is ensuring that you have secured decent, affordable, quality insurance coverage. Health and life insurance are essential to our quality of life and the measures need to be in place when "life" (or rather death) happens. The time to make those decisions is not when a cancer (or other chronic) diagnosis is delivered, or when one is being prepared for death. Do what must be done today in order to secure the protections and coverage for you and your loved ones.

Solid Support System

The fascinating thing about a cancer diagnosis is that it will reveal who is there for you and who does not show up for you in any way. This is not to say that the people who show up for you are the closest, most important people in your life. It could simply mean that they have been given the grace, compassion, wisdom, strength and courage to walk closely with you in this season of sickness. It takes a certain kind of person to decide that they are going to stick with you during the cancer journey. Whether they choose to support you closely (in your personal space) or from a distance with calls, consistent communication, cash or counsel, know that these people will join the ranks of your support system. The close caregivers and family members will become your co-survivors, if/when you conquer this diagnosis. Cherish the ones who choose to embark on the journey with you because although you are experiencing the physical and mental challenges of the diagnosis and treatment, they are also experiencing their own version of mental and emotional anguish.

Many people will not contact you after the diagnosis is revealed. For some, it is their way of giving you space and privacy. People are usually thoughtful and courteous to realize that you will need a certain amount of privacy and personal space as you deal with the sickness. Without being asked, they support quietly by choosing to check in occasionally with caregivers instead of having direct contact with the patient. Some silent supporters may contact once and never reach out again. It doesn't mean they no longer care, but instead it could be their way of acknowledging the diagnosis, then silently supporting you with prayers and staying updated on your progress.

For others, it is their way to deal with the diagnosis in the safety of distance because they are afraid of what it could mean. Fear is an underlying feeling which dictates how people will respond to you. Let me preface this by reminding you that everyone processes sickness in different ways. Some people are not comfortable dealing with chronic sickness, and some are squeamish and scared. Many times, people will stay away, withdraw and avoid interacting with you all together because they are afraid. Their fear is based on two reasons – they are afraid FOR YOU and they are afraid FOR THEMSELVES. People are so conditioned to freeze and go into major panic mode when they hear the word "cancer". In fact, most people don't even like to use the word – it's referred to as "the big C". As a result, when people hear that a loved one or friend has been diagnosed with cancer, they go into the *flight, fright, fight* or *faith* mode (what I called it based on my experience). Depending on which approach they choose to operate from will determine their response towards you.

<u>Flight</u>

These are the people who know you well and have had consistent interaction in your life but are too afraid to stay connected in case you begin to deteriorate rapidly or die, and they can't handle it. They live with the expectation that your death is inevitable and so they distance themselves, avoid all contact and go about their lives as if they don't know you at all. Family and friends may take the "flee" (flight) response, so be prepared in case that happens and it shocks your world. Honestly, this was the hardest part of my journey because I did not expect to feel the rejection, alienation and abandonment that I experienced from certain people. It took me a long time to process those feelings and realize that I should not take their flight personally. It made me question the validity of the many years prior because I wondered if there was any truth and sincerity there. I was not dealing with a common cold, I was diagnosed with cancer, which meant my expectation was that people who had any amount of GOD LOVE and previous affection would still choose to express that during the time of my sickness. That was the biggest shock to my system. That abandonment was much harder to deal with and accept than the cancer. That is one of the things I will have to go to counseling for when all the dust settles because I was left feeling discarded, unloved and abandoned by "Christian" people who should have showed me the authentic love of Jesus in my time of sickness and need.

My encouragement to you is this: if family members, relatives, friends and other loved ones seemingly distance themselves, try not to hold that against them. Most people are not taught the appropriate, affectionate, compassionate and caring ways to respond to someone dealing with cancer. Therefore, people flee to protect themselves and shield their own emotions just in case things don't work out during treatment. You will have no real way of knowing if their reason for leaving is because they don't know how to handle your sickness or if it's just their way of self-protecting. It has nothing to do with you so try to not take it personally or hold it against them because they are operating from a place that requires them to detach in order to safeguard their feelings. I had to learn that lesson the hard way, but in the end, it is ok because the right people will stay.

Fright

These are the people who become so frightened by the situation that it renders them powerless. People who are known to be powerful and dynamic in their public and professional lives become weak and worried when your diagnosis is revealed. Don't misunderstand, it is normal for people to feel worried. In some cases, these people also tend to stay away and have very little contact with you because they don't want you to know how frightened they are. They don't want you to see or hear them crying, so they stay in a constant place of fear which often prevents them from saying or doing anything that could be beneficial to you. Some may reach out once to express their best wishes and promise of prayers just in case you die. For some, it is an obligatory way of feeling that they have paid their respect while you are still alive, just in case death is the outcome. That is ok, many only see a cancer diagnosis as a death sentence and respond to you based on that place of fear and their expectation. Truth be told, you can't blame most persons who respond this way because that is what they are used to. In their minds, a cancer diagnosis indicates a mental preparation for possible death. Regardless of the fearful responses and reactions you may receive from people, try to not take it personally because people are not taught how to deal with this kind of fear. It is no reflection on your worth or your ability to go through the cancer journey successfully; it simply means some people will allow their fear to cripple them and not choose to support you in any way.

Fight

These are the people who hear of the diagnosis and immediately put on their "fighting gloves" for and with you. They are armed with the right words, remedies, resources, and relevant research. The fighters recognize your value and know this is the time to reiterate your overall worth by choosing to fight with and for you. These people don't even entertain the possibility that the diagnosis could end your life; they know it's a possibility, but they choose to not focus on that part. Instead, they make it abundantly clear that they're ready to fight with you until you beat this thing. They willingly offer the gift of presence in the practical tangible ways where it matters most. These are the people who show up to stay with you, transport you when necessary and take care of the practical needs. Fighters use words and positive messages meant to encourage and cheer you on. They are affirming and inspiring. There are also fighters who are not able to be in your physical presence, but they keep in touch, send money to assist with medical and other expenses, arrange for meals to be prepared, pay household bills if necessary and become your support system in the areas where the needs are greatest (especially if you are not able to work and earn a living). Fighters are not delusional about the diagnosis; they simply choose to discard negative thoughts and take the approach that together you will win this fight.

Faith

These are your faith-filled people who not only believe in the power of prayer, but they live lives that reflect their faith. They constantly pray with and for you, not casually but in earnest, believing that God can help, hold and heal you (if He chooses to). These are the people who not only speak or send you Bible verses (if you are a spiritual person), but they also demonstrate faith in their attitude, admonitions, advice and actions towards you. In other words, as my Pastor, Deborah Jackson, often affirms, they don't cancel what they pray with what they say. These are the people who will add your name to prayer lists, get on prayer calls, and schedule people to take turns fasting and praying for you. They expect that you will recover so their prayers are directed towards that outcome. Your faith-filled people also recognize the balance that God is Sovereign and ultimately, His perfect will is desired. They don't manipulate God in their prayers but pray and speak from a place of calm assurance that even during the cancer journey, God can get glory.

Regardless of people's response and reaction to your diagnosis, recognize that it is now a part of your life story and the only response that truly matters is your own! No one gets to choose how you go through the process unless you have invited them to do so (e.g., a caring spouse, parent, grown children). There is no way to predict which persons will have the emotional, mental, financial, and spiritual capacity to respond the way you expect. Therefore, it will do you well to adjust expectations for everyone right now because if you don't, you may end up feeling very disappointed when the people you expect to show up for you choose to handle your diagnosis with indifference, inconvenience, silence and distance. Your only expectation at this point needs to be successfully going through the cancer journey and getting through to the other side, even if the other side means your transition from this life to the next. Your emotional, mental and spiritual energy should be focused on living the best life NOW, even during the health challenge. Because, let's face it, if these are your last weeks, months or years, you want to make sure they are spent in ways that will provide some semblance of a quality life.

In addition, remember that not everyone needs to have access to you while going through your journey. Sometimes, certain people will make things more difficult for you because of their negative attitude, insensitive words and anticipation of doom. It is perfectly ok to avoid interacting and engaging with certain people while you are undergoing treatment because they may do more harm than good. If you choose to fight this cancer battle head-on, know that many will not have the emotional or spiritual capacity to fight with you in their thoughts, actions or even prayers. You are priority number one now more than ever, so even if it means distancing yourself or severing ties from family, friends and folks who are usually involved in some area of your life, do what is necessary for your own good.

Treatment Plans

Power Port Partner

Each person's cancer diagnosis and treatment plan are different and unique to the individual. If you decide to take the traditional treatment (chemotherapy, radiation, surgery–excluding holistic treatment options), then expect to spend quite a bit of time in medical facilities doing various scans, labs and biopsies. My entire body felt violated by the number of times I was poked, probed and required to undergo a variety of testing. Thankfully, most technicians allowed me to play music while a scan or MRI was being administered. As I lay still in the tube, I usually listened to worship music or my favorite album of all time, Yanni's *If I Could Tell You*.

A few days after I was admitted to the hospital, I was wheeled downstairs to surgery for the implantation of the Power Port. I remembered what my daddy's port looked like, so I was not particularly thrilled about that part of the process because in 1990, his port was the kind that bulged and was visible under the skin. Thankfully, things and times have changed, so my power port is flat enough that it is barely visible under the skin.

I understood the necessity of having the port implanted because that was the way I would receive treatment and have blood taken easily and quickly. The Memorial Sloan Kettering Cancer Center (2018) provides the following information on their website about implanted ports:

> An implanted port is a type of central venous catheter (CVC).

An implanted port (also known as a "port") is a flexible tube that's placed into a vein in your chest. It will make it easier for your healthcare team to:

- Give you intravenous (IV, through a vein) medication.
- Give you IV fluids.
- Take blood samples.
- Give you medications continuously for several days. Sometimes medications must be given in a vein larger than the ones in your arms. The port lets the medication go into your bloodstream through a large vein near your heart.

Implanted ports are usually placed about 1 inch (2.5 centimeters) below the center of your right collarbone. If you wear a bra, your implanted port will be about 1 inch from where your bra strap lies. Implanted ports can stay in place for years. Your doctor will remove your port when you don't need it anymore.

Due to the aggressive plan of action that was put in place, I was referred by my oncologist to a specialist at Moffitt Cancer Center in Tampa, Florida. He was known for treating the kind of cancer that I was diagnosed with. Therefore, it was unanimously decided by my medical team that the specialist should see me in person in order to map out the course of treatment. For the first few weeks after the diagnosis, I left my home in Orlando to start treatment at Moffitt in Tampa.

CHAPTER 8

Practical Provisions, Practices & Prayers

I am grateful for friends who knew what to bring when I was
staying at Moffitt and the many other hospital admissions,
because if I was asked what I needed, I had no idea at the time.
Silk pajamas, delicate lingerie and regular bed slippers are not
always the best things to wear during extended hospital stays.
Gowns which facilitate easy access to the port and non-skid socks
with grips are essential. At first, the patient and caregiver may not
know what the practical needs are when preparing for hospitalization. People often say, "Let me know if you need anything." It
is a thoughtful, kind and generous offer from a heart that means
well. However, in the moment, the patient or the loved ones may
not be able to think of the things that are needed, and even if
they do, they may not feel comfortable asking for something if
they do not know what is affordable and feasible for the person
making the offer. Truth be told, it puts additional pressure on
the patient to try and figure out what the specific needs are and
inform people based on limited knowledge of what someone can

provide and afford. My suggestion to those who are thoughtful enough to make that offer is to go ahead and provide something especially if you are not close enough to the patient and loved ones to ask about the specific needs.

In my experience, I was blessed with people who took the initiative and rose to the occasion to provide the things I never even knew I needed. One of my former students (turned brother-friend) started a GoFundMe site and coworkers at PBAU coordinated donation efforts on my behalf. They collected boxes of snacks, food items and gift cards to ensure that while I was in the hospital, basic needs would be covered at home. Church family and friends from near and far blessed me with the kinds of things that would help carry the load. One of the first gifts I received was from a friend in England. She knew that I was a girly girl who enjoyed looking glamorous and gorgeous, so she shipped me a makeup set. Another friend brought a neck pillow and comfortable pajamas. I can't list everything that people gave me, especially during those first weeks, but here are some practical items that you may find useful when preparing for extended hospital stays:

- Toiletries (check with doctors about fragranced products)
- Biotene products for sensitive teeth and sore mouth
- Hospital bag that stays packed in case of unplanned hospital admissions
- Head covering for the bald head (if you lose your hair to chemotherapy)
- Compression socks (swollen feet during and after a long chemotherapy regimen)
- Throws of various sizes (the body is usually cold especially when weight loss occurs)

- Wash rags and towels (I needed my own wash rags once I got home)
- Electric kettle and thermos for the hospital stays
- Snacks and beverages for the hospital stays when you're craving comfort foods
- Boost, Ensure and other nutritional shakes
- Beet juice to help boost the hemoglobin counts (for those daily blood draws)
- Several cases of water to flush the system during chemotherapy
- Disinfectant wipes to regularly clean and sanitize surfaces in the home
- Hand sanitizer for visitors to use and for the patient when in public
- Regular funds for the unexpected expenses related to hospital stays and treatment
- Gas cards for the caregivers who assist with transportation
- People willing to assist with household bills and groceries (if you become unemployed)
- Absorbent diapers (or as I called it, the great exchange)

The Great Exchange–From Victoria's Secret to Depend

Here's the truth that many patients won't tell you. When you are in the hospital receiving ongoing chemotherapy and IV fluids, your bladder works overtime. Preparing for overnight stays or in my case, extended hospital stays as an in-patient, meant there was no need to pack pretty panties (ladies, not even Spanx or the period panties because those will require too much work to remove quickly). Due to the large amount of liquid going into the body, frequent urination becomes a way of life. If you are not strong enough to get out of bed or make it to the toilet fast enough, fit flex absorbent diapers will become your new best friend. In addition, women should pack many maxi pads to use as an additional buffer because you will feel as though your bladder and Kegel exercises are no longer capable of functioning at their usual performance.

Making this kind of adjustment will require some getting used to because it may be necessary to continue wearing absorbent diapers even after you are discharged from the hospital. Being in a weakened state means your body will not be able to move fast enough to get to a bathroom (at home or in public), so always wear protective undergarments until your bladder and physical strength goes back to normal. It became an inside joke when I was out in public with my close friends and proudly announced, (*in my Eartha Kitt voice*) "I'm not wearing Depend" (meaning, I am wearing regular underwear). We laughed about my proud admission, but they understood the significance of those little milestone moments. Hey, It's the truth and somebody's got to tell it like it is – (*In my Sophia voice*: *"You're welcome!"*)

It's Ok to Ask For and Receive Help

When my journey began, I didn't have time to mentally process all the assistance and support I was going to need. I did not realize that every area of my life was going to be impacted and it would require people coming alongside to aid with the most basic tasks and obligations. One of the first things that happened which made me realize that I was going to need others was the initiative taken by my university students and colleagues. They coordinated fundraising efforts (individually and collectively) to assist with medical and life related expenses for those first months. In addition, they donated gift cards, snacks and grocery items so that my children would have enough goodies (especially in my absence). My children really appreciated the many Chick-fil-A gift cards along with other practical restaurant and grocery cards that assisted with household and other essential needs.

As previously indicated, I was blessed and fortunate to have many people (not only my PBAU colleagues) who recognized the need for more than prayer and good wishes and chose to assist me and my family in various ways. Prayers and good wishes were greatly appreciated because that played a significant role in providing spiritual reinforcement for me and my family. However, I also needed practical things to live and take care of my household. I was humbled and overwhelmed by the support that came in tangible and intangible ways especially from people who I would never even think would be so kind and generous. It made me realize that many people who deal with cancer don't get this kind of care because they prefer to embark on their journey privately and with the aid of only a select few. While it is perfectly ok to boldly battle cancer with the help of a few people, I found that it is also brave and beautiful to accept support being offered by others.

Truth be told, I did not know that I would receive this level of assistance because I honestly did not know that I was seen, appreciated and loved in such authentic ways. This revelation was a significant blessing in disguise because God needed to show me that I was indeed loved and cared for by many. I had no idea that the seeds I planted would come back to me and my family in manifold ways. When one gives to others from a pure heart, it is not to get something in return, but to make a positive difference in people's lives (at least that was my motivation through the years). When I asked people why they were being so kind towards me and my family, I was told, "Shannan it's because of who you are and who you have been to others that is causing you to reap the benefits of your own kindness." That blew me away because all through the years, I was oblivious to the impact I had on people's lives. This may sound naïve, and to you it may come across as false humility, but the truth is that I was simply doing what I do and being who I am – not as a perfect person, but as one who strived to be sincere in my motives as it pertained to being supportive of others. I was intentional about influencing, encouraging and inspiring people regardless of the circumstances that allowed our paths to cross. I have always felt that I had a God given, decent human being duty to make sure that my interactions were wholesome, helpful and cheerful. I didn't do any of that to be rewarded by people; I was just being ME! As it turned out, God used the cancer journey to demonstrate that my years of giving to others would come back to me in my time of need. Being blessed and supported by so many people was God's way of making sure I knew that I was truly and deeply loved, valued and cared for.

As the process progressed, I had to become comfortable accepting help without feeling like an encumbrance. I never wanted to be a burden or a bother to anyone, not even my own family. In fact, it was very humbling to admit that I needed assistance to have a bath, walk up the stairs, get groceries at the supermarket, do housework, laundry and even open simple containers (water bottles, lids, etc.) My palms were too frail and sensitive to handle basic tasks. My mother, sister, and brother (Joyce Wallace, Alecia Lewis, Othniel Lewis, respectively) were my biggest blessings in this area because they took turns staying at the home to ensure that things ran smoothly and that the children received care, especially when I was in the hospital. Zaneen Thompson and her sons, Michael and Andre, also stayed at my home sometimes to care for me, provide company and assist with childcare. At the end of an evening visit, my choir sister Latosha Cherry informed our choir director that she would not be singing for a season because she wanted to be available to assist me and the children. Having this kind of presence in the home meant the world to me because none of these people made me feel like a bother or a burden. Their gift of presence played a major role in helping me successfully get through the cancer journey.

I also needed assistance with transportation because there came a point in the process where I was not allowed to drive. Therefore, I had to be chauffeur-driven because my body couldn't handle a motor vehicle and the medications were so strong that my judgment was impaired. In fact, there were times when I would ask the driver to drive at or below the speed limit because I felt anxious at certain speeds. As I am writing this now, I must admit that although I am comfortable driving at rapid speeds, I still feel a sense of caution and anxiety when I am driving more than 65mph on a highway.

When one is used to being independent and in charge, it is very difficult to sit back and accept help from others for just about everything. It was a real adjustment that I had to make, because although I knew there was no stigma and shame in having cancer and needing all the extra assistance, I had to become comfortable embracing all the help I was receiving. That mental switch will require a level of rational, reasonable thinking and maturity so that you will recognize that the assistance and support you need is no reflection on you as an individual. Instead, it means you are going through a major battle and will require care and support from those who truly love you.

Practical Prayers for Cancer Patients

One of the most thoughtful gifts that a cancer patient and their loved ones can receive is prayer. Whether the person is a believer in God or not, most people, when informed of a diagnosis, usually immediately respond with, "My thoughts and prayers are with you." It has become a caring cliché thing to say when a cancer diagnosis is received. There is nothing wrong with that response, especially if it is sincere. One would hope that when people offer and promise to pray, they do so in the moment as well as on other occasions. I am extremely grateful to the many people, prayer groups and churches that were intentional about praying for me and my family. I was informed that some churches even adjusted some of their services to devote time to praying for me. My Tribe sister-friends scheduled days of the week when they took turns fasting and praying so that there was always someone in the WhatsApp group travailing for me. I would not be here today without the many prayers that God heard on my behalf.

Many times, people direct their prayers in the form of demands for healing and miracles with the hope that the patient will not be required to go through the lengthy process of treatment and recovery. The reality is that cancer patients need prayers for more than just a request for healing or a miracle. Prayers are needed for many things, but often people don't know how to pray or what to ask for. I am a firm believer in praying with specificity and inten-sity. In other words, be specific, clear, direct and strategic about what is being asked; pray with your kind of fervor as if you were praying for yourself. It doesn't have to be loud and passionate, but it needs to be sincere, honest and bold. To that end, I made a list of things to pray for when I was in the hospital. In fact, it was one of my most transparent video blogs.

Specific Things to Pray For

- Physical needs as the body and brain fights for survival
- Emotional fortitude to be strong and courageous even in the lowest moments

- Financial obligations for medical and other expenses
- Social needs for appropriate interaction and activities to decrease boredom
- Favorable results for the daily blood draws
- Strength for the veins that are constantly used and weakened
- Neutropenic fevers (shaking chills and high temperature)
- Appropriate treatment plan
- Designated drivers to assist with all transportation needs
- Encouragement from the right kind of people
- Family members being directly impacted
- Caregivers who are constantly caring for the patient

Caring for Your Cancer Patient Family Member/Friend

Don't Do These During or After the Diagnosis:

- Don't withdraw when you find out about a person's diagnosis.
- Don't ask specific questions about the diagnosis and treatment plan unless that information is shared.
- Don't automatically assume that this is a death sentence.
- Don't treat the person like they are no longer useful, relevant or important.
- Don't initiate hugs unless the patient gives permission (low immune system).
- Don't forget to wash hands properly before having physical contact with the patient (home or hospital).
- Don't use the cliché, "If you need anything, let me know."
- Don't compare their cancer diagnosis with someone else's.
- Don't tell them who you know that died from the same kind of cancer.

- Don't disappoint if you set the expectation that you are going to do or give something.
- Don't overwhelm the patient with the research and remedies which may not be relevant in their case.
- Don't have lengthy conversations with the patient as they could become winded.
- Don't send flowers unless you check if the person can have floral items.
- Don't over-spiritualize every conversation or interaction.
- Don't just pray for the patient and then do nothing especially if you have the means to do something.
- Don't assume what the person can eat/drink; ask about dietary needs and restrictions.

ACTION ITEM

Go to Shannan Lewis' Conquering Cancer Journey YouTube Channel and watch the video "How to pray and care for a cancer patient"
https://www.youtube.com/watch?v=ido1KdxyA7U&list=PLC-GMdDzo2F3YOcvYF_XEeMpjNerNTCs4d&index=3

CHAPTER 9

Fatigue Leads To Fall Risk

One of the main indications that the body is experiencing the changes that come with a cancer diagnosis and treatment is extreme weakness. You will feel as though your body is betraying you because even if you feel or look strong, your muscles will indicate otherwise. If you are hospitalized, you will be given a "Fall Risk" bracelet. Don't allow pride to get in the way and cause you to take chances getting out of bed, moving around, and walking without assistance. Your body is changing rapidly and things you are used to doing will become increasingly difficult to undertake.

I will never forget when I passed out in the bathroom at the hospital. I tidied myself and was in the process of brushing my teeth. All I remember after putting on my Depend and preparing to put on my hospital gown, was that I started feeling weak. Thank God I had the presence of mind to pull the red cord on the side of the wall to alert others that I needed help. When I regained consciousness, I was on the floor surrounded by several nurses and technicians attending to me. The reality is that being weak and becoming a fall risk is a part of the process – and that is ok.

There is no reason to feel ashamed or embarrassed because of that new reality.

It is normal to feel as though you are losing your sense of independence because you must rely on people to hold your hand or carry you for your own safety. Resentment may be mixed with embarrassment; annoyance may be accompanied by the feeling that you don't want to be a bother to others. In any case, allow yourself to feel all the emotions that come with navigating this new normal because those feelings are valid. They may not all be true based on your perception and new feelings of insecurity. However, give place to the feelings and put them in proper perspective. You are a fall risk who needs help, not because you are incapable, but you now need the support and care from others to get through what will hopefully be a temporary situation. There is no shame or stigma in sickness, so don't allow yourself to feel as though the need for assistance is something to be embarrassed about.

Don't allow the diagnosis and debilitating conditions to define or diminish you. Just because your limbs and legs are weak does not negate the strength you still possess on the inside. You are still YOU – fabulous, strong, resilient, creative, courageous, determined, unique, precious, valuable, and irreplaceable. Cancer may take a lot from you, but it cannot take your spirit if you don't relinquish it. Although your body feels weak and there are other things happening which may cause you to be deemed disabled, don't lose sight of who you are at your core. The process may not be what you want, and it may be harder than you imagine, but the diagnosis does not have to be the determining factor that speaks to who you are as an individual.

Once I realized that I was constantly wobbly and weak, it took everything in me to force my mind to remember that I was still strong on the inside. There were times when my fingertips were too frail and I was not strong enough to write or my vision was too blurry to read, but it did not change the fact that I was still sharp, smart and savvy. Chemo brain was not going to allow me to forget who I was, neither was I going to give in to the effects of medication and act as though I was no longer useful. Wisdom and my doctors dictated that I had to be deemed disabled because of the new physical limitations and restrictions, but I was not going to give in to that description and own it permanently (unless that was what the Lord wanted). I had to recognize what the cancer could not do and that included destroying my sense of self and my value. While waiting to get my labs done one day, I read the following on the wall as the nurse prepared to take my blood. This was very helpful once I recognized how true it was:

What Cancer Cannot Do

It cannot cripple LOVE
It cannot shatter HOPE
It cannot destroy PEACE
It cannot kill FRIENDSHIPS
It cannot suppress MEMORIES
It cannot silence COURAGE
It cannot invade the SOUL
It cannot steal ETERNAL LIFE
It cannot conquer THE SPIRIT

CHAPTER 10

Chemotherapy

The treatment plan for each person's cancer diagnosis is determined by various factors. The medical team considers the type of cancer, the results from lab work, the progression (some cancers are detected early enough to treat while others are discovered when the person is almost close to dying). In my case, the type of cancer meant an aggressive approach was required. According to the Cancer Treatment Centers of America (2019):

> Most cancers are staged based on the size and spread of tumors. However, because leukemia already occurs in the developing blood cells in the bone marrow, leukemia staging is a little bit different. The stages of leukemia are often characterized by blood cell counts and the accumulation of leukemia cells in other organs, like the liver or spleen. Making an educated treatment decision begins with the stage, or progression, of the disease. The stage of **leukemia** is one of the most important factors in evaluating treatment

options. Factors affecting **leukemia** staging and prognosis include:

- White blood cell or platelet count
- Age (advanced age may negatively affect prognosis)
- History of prior blood disorders
- Chromosome mutations or abnormalities
- Bone damage
- Enlarged liver or spleen

My mom, sister, brother and I were given the harsh reality that I would be given chemotherapy and radiation. Being young and healthy gave my doctors the confidence that the prescribed treatment plan would work. They were optimistic that I had a good chance of being receptive to treatment and recovery. Once the cancer was no longer detected in my system, a bone marrow transplant would be needed in order to extend my life and increase the chance of it never returning.

Most people automatically associate a cancer diagnosis with the dreaded chemotherapy that is often used as an integral part of the treatment plan. Although it is an effective way to kill fast growing cancer cells in the body, many people don't look forward to the actual process because while it is designed to do good, it is accompanied by several side effects and negative risks. The American Cancer Society explains that:

> Chemo drugs kill fast-growing cells, but because these drugs travel throughout the body, they can affect normal, healthy cells that are fast-growing, too. Damage to healthy cells causes side effects. More than 100 **chemotherapy** or chemo drugs

are used to treat cancer – either alone or in combination with other drugs or treatments. These drugs are very different in their chemical composition, how they are taken, their usefulness in treating specific forms of cancer, and their side effects. (2019)

Consequently, there is usually some level of hesitation and trepidation when a patient and their loved ones are informed that chemotherapy will be used in the treatment plan.

Such was the case with me and my loved ones, mainly because we saw what chemotherapy did to my dad. Not only did he lose all his hair, but his nails and skin became dark, he was frequently ill, and the weight loss caused him to look gaunt and frail. However, since my medical team took the time on several occasions to educate us and explain the severity of the situation, we realized that chemotherapy would have to begin and continue until the results were attained and remission was achieved.

Armed with information about the process and the potential side effects, I mentally and spiritually prepared for this phase of the battle. Once I was assured by my nurses that I would still be able to watch Netflix, post on social media and interact with others while the chemo drugs were being administered, I relaxed and allowed myself to get comfortable. Being able to maintain some semblance of control and normalcy during the process was helpful to my psyche. In fact, during those initial chemo sessions, I was able to sit up in bed or on the sofa in my room and do work for the university. Technically, I was still employed because I was out on **Family and Medical Leave Act – FMLA**. The ability to do my makeup, put on a wig, enjoy music and just be myself during the administration of chemotherapy, was beneficial to my overall attitude and feeling about the process. Granted, it wasn't always easy, but it allowed me to maintain some amount of control.

Unlike many cancer patients who receive their chemo as an out-patient (they go in at a designated time and sit in a room with other patients for the duration of the treatment), my chemo regimen required admission to the hospital as an in-patient. Several of the drugs being administered lasted for many hours, which meant I was not able to leave the hospital and return home. Hence, my chemo days were usually 4–7 days in the hospital every 3 or 4 weeks.

Most people detest the chemotherapy process because of the way it affects the person's body. According to The American Cancer Society (2019), the most common side effects of chemotherapy include:

- Fatigue
- Hair loss
- Easy bruising and bleeding
- Infection
- Anemia (low red blood cell counts)
- Nausea and vomiting
- Appetite changes
- Constipation
- Diarrhea
- Mouth, tongue, and throat problems such as sores and pain with swallowing
- Nerve and muscle problems such as numbness, tingling, and pain
- Skin and nail changes such as dry skin and color change
- Urine and bladder changes and kidney problems
- Weight changes
- Chemo brain, which can affect concentration and focus

- Mood changes
- Changes in libido and sexual function
- Fertility problems

Although the possible side effects were not what I would have wanted, I had to stay in fight mode by choosing to acknowledge that this was integral to the healing and recovery journey. As a person of faith, I had to believe that God already knew that this was coming and if He chose this path, I had to embrace it and His plan for my medical treatment. I was assured that only time would tell which side effects would impact me in the short and long term. The fact is, not every patient gets all the side effects. That is revealed once the process begins so that the patient, care-givers and medical team can respond accordingly.

The prayer warrior in me chose to maintain some semblance of control by acting in faith. To that end, each time the nurses brought the chemo bags to my room, I asked them to let me hold it so that I could pray and tell it what it could do and what it was not allowed to do. I calmly said with every ounce of faith in me, "***Go in and do only what you are supposed to do. Do not infiltrate any other area or affect any organs. I want minimal side effects. Do your job then get the hell out of my system!***" Somehow, talking out loud to the chemo bags was my way of accepting that although the treatment was meant to help me, I was not going to give in and allow it to diminish, deplete or destroy me.

No chemo drug was administered until a group of nurses confirmed the patient's name and medical information on the order. The chemotherapy treatment was prepared by the pharmacist with certain specifications, so they had to confirm as a group, then have me verbally confirm my information every single time to ensure that the right patient was receiving the right chemo in the right order.

During and after a chemo week, I looked and felt like Humpty Dumpty because of the amount of fluid that was pumped in my body. Some people may have thought I was gaining weight from the photos I shared on social media. But in reality, the cheeks and legs were so puffy and swollen, that I looked heavier, not due to rapid weight gain but the chemo drugs and other IV fluids. In order to ensure that the extra fluid rapidly left my body, it was necessary to urinate frequently. To that end, I had to constantly flush my system by drinking several bottles of water each day. It was so serious that I used to keep more than 10 bottles of water in my bedroom at home just so that I could have them within easy reach.

ACTION ITEM

For more details pertaining to the staging and
grading of leukemia, visit
https://www.cancercenter.com/cancer-types/eukemia/stages

CHAPTER 11

Hair Loss

I didn't begin to lose my hair until about a month after chemotherapy treatment began. Being in and out of the hospital with new skin sensitivities and precautions meant that I could no longer shave as a part of my usual grooming. The last thing I needed was to put myself at risk using a razor, tweezer or any other means to control hair growth. I kept asking the nurses when they believed I would start losing my hair, because to me, THAT would certainly indicate that the chemo drugs were moving around in my body and doing what they were supposed to do. No one could accurately predict when I would start losing my hair, so I kept my "Set It Off" cornrows under my weave. (See Queen Latifah's hairstyle in the "Set It Off" movie if you are not familiar.) Somehow, I thought that should be "safe" until the hair started falling and I would have a "Shave the head" party with my close friends (at least that was the way I thought it was going to happen).

My expectation was that I would start losing hair from my head and so would begin the hair loss process, but NO, my body (and God) had other plans. During a trip to the bathroom in my hospital room, I realized that my Depend underwear was "decorated". With a somewhat clueless puzzled look, I proceeded to handle my business (frequent urination was the norm). But when my short purpose for using the toilet was completed, I was both amused and aghast at the sight of hair mixed in with the urine. I literally laughed out loud and said, "God, you truly have a sense of humor." My hair loss began in my most intimate, private place.

Shortly thereafter, I scheduled an appointment at Studio Glam with Kat Jackson, my hair stylist (and friend) to wash and redo my hair with a quick weave (i.e., glue the weave onto a stocking cap and place it on the head like a wig). I figured seeing that I still had hair on my head, why not get a cute hairstyle? Although I was undergoing cancer treatment, I still wanted to look and feel glamorous and gorgeous. While I sat in her chair, as she combed with little effort, my hair started coming out in large clumps. Apparently, it started breaking away from the scalp but was hidden in the "Set If Off" cornrows, so I had no idea that the head hair loss had also begun. Later, Kat admitted that after I left her salon, she cried for me because the sign of hair loss made my cancer diagnosis real for her.

That weekend I went out to eat with my siblings, supported my daughter at a school concert and went to church for the first time since the cancer diagnosis. To use a popular contemporary phrase, "I was feeling myself" for the first time in a long time. A woman's hair is such an important part of her identity, so being able to go out in public with a nice new hairstyle meant the world to me.

On Sunday March 9, 2017, I went to church with my family and was warmly welcomed by my River of Life Christian Center family. It was the first Sunday that I was able to go to church since the January diagnosis, so I was very excited. Even though I had to put on my mask before entering the building, I did not mind because I missed being with my worship leaders, choir members and church family. The worship and warmth of my church family meant the world to me.

After a dynamic church service, my siblings and I returned to Allie's home for Sunday dinner and sibling bonding. On the way home, I asked Otty and Allie if we could sing together when we arrived at the house. We often sing whenever we are together. In many ways, it reminds us of our Lewis Legacy because our parents sang together and encouraged singing at home and at church when we were children. Honestly, at the time, I made the request because I was cognizant of the possibility that each time we were together, we had to maximize those moments in case it would be our last.

My siblings obliged me as we sat at the piano and sang "Deliver You" which was written by Allie and arranged by Otty (a professional musician). I am so glad that I recorded that moment because a few hours later, things got real (again). Otty left to run an errand so Allie and I settled in on the sofa to watch TV. To protect my new hairstyle, I used a colorful head scarf to cover my head because I usually fall asleep while watching TV on Allie's sofa. For some reason, I ran my fingers along the front hairline of my head. Immediately, Allie screamed, "Jesus, Jesus, Jesus...yu hair, your hair!!!" It took me a few seconds to comprehend what she was seeing and saying – my head scarf came off my head with the quick weave, revealing major hair loss. Apparently, my hair was gone so there was no longer any grip to keep my weave hairstyle in place. As I grabbed my phone and started taking photos to see exactly what it looked like, I thought to myself, "Thank God this didn't happen at church a few hours ago." I had no way of knowing that my hair was mostly gone but the loss was hidden. The cornrows had matted and locked creating a strange looking "design".

In the moment I was too fascinated to feel the fear that was rising to the surface. Somehow although I knew that the head hair loss was going to be a significant part of the journey, when it happened I was filled with mixed emotions so it was hard to process everything that afternoon. "So much for the 'Shave my head' party that I was hoping to have," I thought, and resigned myself to the new reality. At that rate, it appeared that the hair was disappearing quickly and there would be no time to mark the moment with my close girlfriends. That afternoon made it official – chemotherapy took my hair!

Watching my hair "take wings" each week felt surreal. As a grown-up glamorous, gorgeous girly girl, my hairstyles were always integral to my identity. I have been known to wear and rock various stylish short cuts, braids, twists, weaves and wigs. Losing my hair threatened to attack a big part of my identity as a fabulous, fierce female.

However, the fighter within knew better than to give in to those feelings of insecurity and inadequacy. I had to find the strength to affirm myself as I watched the changes occur. I had to see pass the hair loss on my head, underarms, pubic area, eyelashes, eyebrows, legs and arms and STILL recognize that I was so much more than my hair. I had to see the changing skin, the darkening of the nails, the bags under my eyes, the blurry vision and all the other things that were beginning to manifest due to chemotherapy treatment. I had to see that I was still SHANNAN and I was worthy of love, care and support.

CHAPTER 12

Rules, Restrictions, & Routines

D ealing with cancer means adhering to new rules, restrictions and routines to ensure that the patient and caregivers take extra precaution to minimize risks. They can sometimes feel like an inconvenience or annoyance, but following the rules, restrictions and routines must become a part of one's lifestyle for the sake of protection. Cancer Treatment Centers of America (2019) states, "...precautions aren't merely a seasonal consideration, but a constant reality, because catching an infection is more than a minor inconvenience—it could have serious implications for their health and treatment schedule." I learned very quickly in the cancer journey that pride had to take a back seat for wisdom to dictate my adherence to the new ways I had to live. Self-protection and preservation meant ignoring feelings of self-consciousness and not wondering what people thought about me when I had to venture out in public or sanitize immediately if someone touched my hand. The following are rules and routines that became a way of life during the process.

Masks

Wearing masks is mandatory whenever the patient is not at home (and may even be required if someone in the home has a cough or illness). The goal is to provide a protective shield for the nose and mouth to minimize the risk of airborne bacteria and breathing in other people's air. Most medical facilities and hospitals provide masks, but they can also be purchased at pharmacies. When the patient is home and interacting with others who may be fighting a cold, allergies or anything that results in a cough or sneeze, the sick person (family member or visitor) should also wear a mask to reduce the possibility of droplets falling on surfaces that the patient could come in contact with later. Personally, I did not like the fact that I had to be seen in public with a mask covering most of my face, but I could not allow pride and feeling self-conscious to cause me to take chances. Frankly, I got used to it so that after a while, it didn't bother me at all. I understood how important that protective layer was even if it meant people could not see my lips curl into a smile. My hope was that people would see the smile in my eyes and the hope in my heart.

Hand Hygiene

Frequent hand washing and using hand sanitizer must become a regular routine to minimize the risk of picking up germs. Having a lower immune system means the body is more susceptible to infections from touching surfaces like door handles, counter tops, light switches and just about any surface that is touched by multiple people. In my home, we stocked up on disinfectant wipes and regularly sanitized surfaces to ensure that if/when I came in contact with those areas, I would not get germs.

Avoid Large Crowds

Due to the possibility of getting sick from airborne bacteria, it is best to avoid being in crowded places. Supermarkets, shopping malls, places of worship and even public swimming pools should be avoided especially during the initial phase of treatment. If one has to go to these places, a mask must be worn and there should be little or no direct contact with people, i.e., no touching, hugging or hand shaking. The social butterfly that I am had a hard time accepting this rule/restriction even though I had no choice but to adhere. It was very difficult not to be able to attend church regularly because that's where I usually received my weekly fuel (corporate worship, the Word and the warmth of welcoming, loving people). Even though I was able to watch the church services via LiveStream, I felt isolated not being able to interact in person. Needless to say, once I got the permission to attend from time to time, I wore my mask and informed my church family that I could only give and receive air-hugs.

Head Covering

Losing one's hair during chemotherapy results in a cold, bald head. That was one of the most surprising things that I experienced. I assumed that I would be able to wear my bald head in public and feel totally cute and comfortable, but that was not the case. My head felt cold all the time, even at home. Thankfully, I had several warm knit beanie caps, head scarves and a variety of stylish headwear that kept my head covered. I was quite amused at the irony which took place once I lost my hair. I had little desire to wear wigs. Even though I was used to wearing wigs prior to the cancer journey, I enjoyed not feeling like I needed to wear them while going through the cancer chemo experience.

Throws and Blankets

Cancer patients usually feel cold even in normal temperatures. I learned very quickly that I could not be without a warm jacket, soft throw or blanket even in public places. If I dared leave the house without a jacket, I would hear a dear friend in my mind asking, "Where's your jacket young lady?" (in that unmistakable loving big sister tone of voice). In fact, all of my sister-caregivers always made sure there was something warm within reach that I could use to wrap around myself. I fondly recall sitting in a church service and having my sister-friend-neighbor look at me, then reach for my throw to wrap around my shoulders. In the online newsletter "Medical News Today," Christian Nordqvist explains that "humans with **cancer** are more susceptible to **feeling cold** in 'normal' temperatures, especially after receiving treatment" (2013).

Sharing the Toilet

In my home, we established a rule that no one was allowed to use my toilet, as was the case for my bathroom in the hospital. After a chemotherapy regimen, the urine had a distinct odor which I detested. In order to flush the chemo from my body quickly, I drank several bottles of water daily. This meant that I could not take the chance of someone using my bathroom when I needed to "make a run for it", or rather, do a slow walk-run to the "throne". (Did you visualize my slow walk-run?) It was best to keep my bathroom clean and available at all times. In addition, the chemicals in chemotherapy were so strong that it was almost like poison. Hence, it was not wise to allow others to use the toilet that I used for their own safety.

<u>Shaving</u>

During cancer treatment, I chose to stop shaving to reduce the risk of cutting myself and bleeding due to sensitive skin. But once all my body hair was gone, it became a non-issue. An article from the <u>Mayo Clinic </u>(https://www.mayoclinic.org/tests-proce-dures/chemotherapy/in-depth/hair-loss/art-20046920) explains:

> Chemotherapy may cause hair loss all over your body-not just on your scalp. Sometimes your eyelash, eyebrow, armpit, pubic and other body hair falls out." If you're actively undergoing che-motherapy- or radiation-related treatments, it's best to stop waxing and shaving altogether... if radiation therapy causes your skin to become red, irritated or inflamed, resist the urge to wax or shave until the skin is completely healed." (CV SkinLabs, 2009)

As I write this, my hair is back but I still take precautions when shaving, especially my underarms because of the surgical scar. Furthermore, the skin is still a tender part of my body that I have to treat with more care now than I did before cancer.

CHAPTER 13

Nutritional Needs

I am finally prepared to admit to the world (well, YOU the reader) that I am a foodie! (DEEP BREATH...AUDIBLE SIGH). I feel relieved at that admission (and please don't judge me). Prior to cancer, I had no idea that I was a mood eater who used food for comfort and to appease boredom. I was never one of those ladies who was a picky eater, always measuring and counting calories, reading labels and depriving myself for the sake of looking thin. More power to those who are disciplined about everything they eat! That wasn't my main priority. I ate well and healthy, not overly indulging, but using moderation and my own desires as the motivating factors. Food was a gift from God, and I was a grateful recipient who had a healthy appetite. Here's the thing though, one never realizes how much they love or depend on food until it cannot be consumed or enjoyed. Such was the case when my appetite and taste buds decided to go into rebellion mode while I was developing dry mouth from chemotherapy. It was enough to make this decent Christian girl almost cuss (ALMOST!!!). I did not expect the changes that took place once chemo treatments began. Not only was I given a long list of things I could and could not eat/drink, but my body was not cooperating at all. I was not pleased! This foodie was ticked off and not appreciating that part of the journey.

Nutrition before, during and after cancer treatment is an essential part of the process because the body needs all the help it can get to maintain health, strength and weight. Many cancer patients experience drastic weight loss during the process due to the inability to eat meals and keep foods down. Liquid diets usually become a main source of receiving necessary nutrients, such as calories and protein. For me, supplements like Ensure and Boost became one of my main sources of a full healthy meal because it was hard to eat or enjoy meals.

During the initial stages of chemotherapy, I was able to eat and enjoy a variety of healthy Jamaican meals. In fact, my former Worship Center church sister, Donna Grant, worked at the hospital and bought Jamaican meals for me on several occasions. Some mornings, she would stop at a Jamaican restaurant to bring me breakfast if I sent her a text message before she left for work. My mother frequently made a variety of delicious home-cooked meals and vegetable drinks which I enjoyed in the hospital. Thankfully, there was a refrigerator in the room which allowed me to store my meals and beverages. However, as the treatment progressed and my body got the memo that changes were taking place, side effects arrived on schedule and it became more difficult to indulge in my favorite food items. It was a sad day when I was forced to accept that Jamaican food tasted different, but it was even sadder when I almost choked trying to chew and swallow bread. Dry mouth took over and my saliva glands seemingly disappeared. Foods would ball up in my mouth and struggle to go down my throat. It was one of the most annoying experiences because it meant my diet had to be restricted to soft foods like applesauce, popsicles, broth and protein drinks.

Unlike most people who endure horrible nausea and vomiting as a result of chemotherapy, I didn't have that experience during the first regimens. However bothersome side effects made it difficult to enjoy food and I had to turn in my "foodie" card. I was not pleased, I was angry and I was hungry (HANGRY!!!).

Decreased immunity leads to dietary guidelines which must be followed to protect the patient from bacteria in foods and food preparation. When one's immune system is significantly compromised, there is a greater risk for infection from the seemingly simple things. It wasn't enough for me to properly wash and consume raw fruits and vegetables (things that I thoroughly enjoyed). This foodie loved all kinds of fruits and salads (the more ingredients, the better). Sadly, I had to give up those things in the first few weeks of the diagnosis. This was one of the first restrictions placed on me once the cancer-chemo journey began. I had to prepare a list of DOs and DON'Ts that was kept on my home refrigerator as a reminder for myself and caregivers:

Avoid Eating

Raw fruits and vegetables
Eggs with runny yolks
Deli meats
Raw nuts/seeds
Raw or undercooked meats
Pre-made salads (potato salad, pasta salad, tuna salad)
Undercooked fish
Fountain drinks, smoothies or any drink made from a juice bar
Lemon or lime slices
Iced beverages
Ice from restaurants, bagged ice or from self-serve machines
Chinese take-out foods

All-you-can-eat restaurants
Food prepared that was left uncovered for any amount of time

Allowed Foods

Meats cooked well-done
Eggs that are well cooked
Dairy products made from pasteurized milk
Cooked vegetables
Sodas in can or bottle
Nutritional shakes

Is it any wonder that cancer patients lose weight rapidly? With limited diet and restrictions, coupled with the loss of appetite and the changes in the way food tastes, additional measures need to be considered to assist with nutritional needs. Now remember that this is not the case for everyone doing the cancer-chemo journey; this was my experience. While in the hospital, I was assigned a nutritionist to help me with dietary needs to ensure that I was still getting enough nutrients and supplements. She would make sure that the cafeteria staff brought me several Ensure protein drinks each day, in addition to providing an update of my dietary needs and restrictions.

CHAPTER 14

Parking Permit Privilege

It took me a while before I accepted that it was time to go to the Department of Motor Vehicles (DMV) to get a disabled parking permit. Do you recall when I previously indicated that a cancer patient can sometimes feel betrayed by the body because of the weakness in the limbs? Well, that was the case for me because I still looked somewhat strong but everything below the waist yelled and pretty much cussed at me whenever I tried to walk any distance (even short distances). My legs went into straight revolt especially if I drove for any amount of time and had to get out of the car after driving. Therefore, it became obvious that I needed to park as close to buildings as I could before my legs gave way and threatened to embarrass me in public. To avoid the possible humiliation, especially when I did not have someone to hold my hand and help me to walk, I took advantage of the official indicator that I was now considered disabled.

As was the case with navigating each new normal in this process, I had to put it in proper perspective. A disabled parking permit is a privilege provided to those who legitimately need to be parked close to buildings in order to shorten the walk time.

Instead of being stubborn, resentful or seeing this as something to feel ashamed of, I accepted that this too was now a part of my reality. Years later, I still use the parking privilege because sometimes it still takes a few seconds for my body to get its bearings. I still have moments when my body reminds me that I am not 100% back to normal and sometimes my legs still send the message that I should not try to walk long distances. Consequently, being able to park in the designated disabled parking spot is a blessing in disguise that I did not know a cancer diagnosis was going to provide. For the most part, I use regular parking spots, but it is certainly a blessing to know that if I need to park close to a building, I have a legitimate right to do so. Thankfully, there is a time limit on the permit which means that it will expire in July 2021.

Seeing that I am on the subject, let me caution you that there are people who speak before they think and will try to accuse you of parking in a disabled parking spot yet "there's nothing wrong with you". I have had people mention that to me and ask that I remove my car based on their assumption that I looked fine and didn't need the parking privilege. Let this be a reminder to the readers that we have no idea why a doctor would give written authorization for a person to receive a disabled parking permit. A person can look healthy and strong on the outside yet is dealing with health challenges that are not visible or known to others. Therefore, we should be respectful of people who choose to park in a disabled spot with a legitimate parking permit displayed.

CHAPTER 15

Impact on the Children

A cancer diagnosis affects minor children in ways that the patient and other family members may not be aware of initially. From the moment that I realized this was not a dream or a short process, my main motivation for conquering the disease was the fact that I have young children. Having lost my own father to cancer shortly after I had turned 17 years old, meant that my siblings and I had to grow up without our dad during those tricky, tumultuous teenage years. Navigating life was difficult but it wasn't until I got older that I realized how much we were affected by the loss of our dad. Consequently, I pleaded with God not to allow the same thing to happen to my children. When I was diagnosed, my daughter, Shanel, was 15 years old and my son, Daniel, turned 11 years old a few days after the diagnosis. There was nothing that could have prepared the children for the ways in which their life was going to change as a result of the cancer diagnosis and journey. Regular routines were disrupted, fear took up residence and the feeling that they had to be strong overwhelmed their minds. It's annoying that sickness comes without warning which means it does not provide the time or space to prepare. There are no indicators that signal children to mentally adjust to the fact that their childhood is about to be diverted.

Looking back, I had no way of knowing that when cancer invaded my life it would wreak havoc on my children, meaning their entire world was also turned upside and fear became their dominant emotion. Like me, Shanel and Daniel were also minding their business, going about the "regularly scheduled program" of school-aged kids, when they got the news that Mommy was in the hospital and would not be coming home for a little while. Imagine the many questions that must have bombarded their 15- and 11-year-old minds? "Is Mommy going to be sick all the time?" "Can I get and receive hugs from Mommy?" "Is Mommy going to die soon?" Try to envision the anxiety that made normal, somewhat semi-carefree thinking a thing of the past for the children.

Our regular routines were interrupted without warning and I was angry!!! Yes, I accepted that this was now a part of our life story and God had me on assignment, but I was ticked off that cancer dare invade our mommy-kids space!! I was furious that my children were going to have to deal with this crap as if they hadn't already had a challenging life. My children lived through lack, loss and little bit because financially, things were never what it was supposed to be. They experienced car repossessions, a house foreclosure, and regular school changes so much that the theme of loss became prevalent in their lives. I did not want them to deal with another loss so soon after everything that had just happened in previous years. I was annoyed that they would have many fears, questions and concerns and would be unable to articulate those things appropriately. I was pissed off (yes, I just wrote pissed off) because my mommy life lessons were not finished as I had so much more to teach them.

My parents set the example of the practical life skills that must be taught to children in the home. Mommy taught us how to clean and maintain a house (my siblings and I had assigned chores as early as 5 years old). She made sure we knew how to sew, do laundry, cook complete meals and do grocery shopping (all before we were in our late teens). Daddy was a hands-on head of household who set the example of how to lead a family by demonstrating how certain life skills should be done. In fact, it was my daddy who taught me how to iron a shirt, make a bed, make a budget, set a schedule, do bank transactions and pay bills. It was Daddy who had the first "birds and bees" puberty conversation with me when my little breasts started feeling like tennis balls. Needless to say, I wanted to continue teaching the life lessons and skills that were an integral part of the way I cared for my children. I had started teaching and modeling those essential life skills to the children and was nowhere close to completing those lessons. I was angry that cancer had the nerve to come and interrupt my mommy ministry and main mission in life at that time.

This interruption and invasion meant there was...

- *no more "special order, special order" breakfast (my favorite phrase from the movie "Ratatouille" when I wanted to find out what they wanted to eat or inform them that a meal was ready to be devoured)*
- *no more banana fritters that they could eat any time of the day (because I knew how much they liked this Jamaican dish)*
- *no warm hugs after the evening arrival from school and work (because my immune system was compromised, and I had to avoid hugging)*
- *no mommy-kids time in my bed watching "Black-ish" and our favorite DVR recorded shows*
- *no more trips to the pool, the gym or even the Chinese buffet close to our home*

- *no oatmeal supper before bedtime or the after-midnight comfort food requests because they are night owls who enjoyed my mommy treats after hours*
- *no one to adjust the worship music playing in the living room so that it was loud enough to seep into their sub-conscious as they slept, but soft enough not to disturb sweet dreams*
- *no more walking through the house late at night praying, anointing and singing worship songs over them as they slept*

I wanted to protect my children from all that lay ahead, yet all I knew to do in those moments was to love them as usual with my daily WhatsApp messages, phone calls, air hugs and air kisses, regular inquiries and prayers. I was more pissed off about what the sickness would do to the children than what it could do to me. How the heck was I supposed to be the mother that I strive to be if I was not able to be as present as I usually was? How was I supposed to go in their rooms at night and adjust their covers and check their beds to make sure there were no pencils that remained after they finished homework in the bed? How the heck was I supposed to anoint them with olive oil and pray quietly as they slept if I was stuck in a hospital room? Who the dickens gave permission for my kids to have to take on such strength and act like this sickness was something they could handle? Who signed off on that???? *(Insert angry, not-so-Christian words because I am triggered as I'm writing this)*. My momma bear was not pleased because my highest calling in life (apart from being God's grateful girl) is being their mother and I could not protect them from the disruption of the diagnosis!!! I can't recall if I cussed during the process, but if I did, I know God understood that language and forgave the mother in me who wanted to protect her babies from this cruel, intrusive disease.

Anyway, (LONG AUDIBLE SIGH) instead of going off on God, I saw my children as the real motivation for why I should fight and conquer the sickness. Shanel and Daniel became my real medicine, my why, my reason, and my main motivation to conquer cancer and live well. I knew what my assignment was in their lives because I knew they were going to be born years before I was even married. When I was a teenager, I had a dream that I was going to have a daughter named Shanel and a son we called DJ. In the dream, Shanel was born on a Sunday evening and that night her grandfather announced to the congregation that she was born that evening. Sure enough, many years later Shanel skipped her due date and arrived on a Sunday evening as the sounds of Cece Winans' "It Wasn't Easy, But It Was Worth It" played in the delivery room. Years later, I was visiting a church in Orlando. At the end of the service, the pastor, who had never met me, came to me and said, "What do you mean you've locked shop?" (Meaning, why aren't you trying to get pregnant again?). He continued to prophesy saying, "You have a son in there and you need to give him the names of prophets." Shortly after, DJ was born and we named him Daniel Joshua.

I used to talk to my children and pray for them even when they were in my womb. My awareness of my mommy ministry was more than the usual expectations of breastfeeding, nourishment, comfort and motherly care. I knew that I was anointed and appointed to prepare my children to be good citizens of the world and image bearers of Jesus Christ. I knew that I was authorized to make decisions concerning their wellbeing which would ensure that their being was well (spiritually, socially, emotionally, mentally and physically). I knew how to balance being fun, firm and fair without over-emphasizing one method over others. I knew how to identify and articulate personality traits, characteristics and inclinations that were both positive and negative, and I had no hesitation calling out those things that reflected negative generational patterns and praying against them. I knew I needed to stick around longer to prepare them for the tricky, tough, turbulent teenage years and escort them into adulthood as the coach/cheerleader mom who gives them space to make their own decisions but remains accessible when they need me. To that end, I made sure the doctors, nurses, housekeepers and pretty much anyone who was a regular part of my medical team, knew my children by their names and photos. I made sure that their photos were displayed in the hospital room because I intended to live for myself and my babies.

I was very careful not to give the children the raw real facts about the diagnosis, especially in the first few days. As far as they knew, Mommy was still not feeling well (remember I was being treated for bronchitis). Life and lengthy conversations through the years with the children taught me how to be sensitive about sharing too much too soon (and this goes for all things pertaining to conduct and communication with children). However, once they visited the Oncology floor of the hospital, I knew that these two intelligent beings would possibly do a Google search for the word "Oncology" and figure out that Mommy wasn't staying there because she was being treated for bronchitis. Needless to say, this led to an honest conversation that no manual, no Bible, no person and nothing gave me the rules about how to tell your young children that you have cancer. But I could not insult their intelligence, ignore what they were curious about or imply that this was a little thing that would quickly be resolved. I had (and still do) a relationship with my children that provided the sanctity and safety of transparency and vulnerability. Although they were minors, we had developed a rapport that allowed us to have "keep it real" conversations that were fluid, meaning they could candidly share with me and I could do the same with them (in proper age appropriate context and within reason). It was within this framework of love, honesty and mutual respect that I shared the diagnosis. I didn't want to give that task to someone else because we had an established mommy-kids relationship and not even cancer was going to change that dynamic. I loved and respected them enough to tell them the truth and deliver it in a way that they would see and hear hope, faith and courage in my eyes and voice.

Once they saw that I was going to fight the battle and intended to win, it enabled them to approach the cancer journey with cautious optimism that together we were going to get through this. To that end, they did homework and had dinner in my hospital room, ignored me while socializing on their devices like normal pre-teens and teens do, and tried their best to interact with me as usual whenever they visited. I was adamant not to have them visit too often though because I did not want it to become too much for them to deal with, especially when I was not having a good day. However, whenever I was home, we tried to maintain as much routine as possible. They rose to the occasion and assisted me with walking because my body was often too weak to move around as I used to do before. Daniel was used to asking, "Mom, do you need anything?" before I got sick, but he took his attention to another level during those months. He often paused from homework or gaming to lay his hands on me and pray quietly or climb in bed with me for company and comfort. Shanel was always ready to serve as she made sure I was lacking nothing if I needed a warm blanket, a hot cup of tea or a favorite snack. Although they were attentive and caring, I never wanted them to feel as though they had to take care of me – no mother ever wants to put her children in that position. However, the cancer journey provided the children many opportunities to demonstrate love in more than words; they were being taught how to love in action. The cancer journey taught my children how to show concern, compassion, and care while cherishing, honoring and extending love towards a sick loved one. No textbook, movie or even church sermon could teach them that. They had to go through the experience to gain that knowledge and understanding of what it really means to love in the context of family.

Being hospitalized meant I had to figure out how to mother them from a distance (proximity, not the heart) while safeguarding their emotions. It required a delicate balance of maintaining mommy roles and responsibilities while recognizing the need to interact and share information in measured doses that was age appropriate. For Shanel and Daniel, it meant holding anxiety, fears, questions, confusion and anger in places that would emerge and manifest later. Time would tell the tale of how the diagnosis, medical treatment and people's responses affected my children. My mommy prayers at that time were that they would be given the grace, strength, courage and right people to go through the journey, because it became obvious to me that this was going to be an integral part of their own life stories and testimonies. The Lord was gracious enough to remind me that He kept me and my siblings and gave us powerful testimonies even though Daddy dealt with and eventually died because of cancer. I realized that my children had their own pathway to walk and dealing with this situation was going to help shape the people they were going to be. With that assurance, I rested in God's promise that this would also be a way for Him to get glory in their lives and that this would set them up for greatness.

My children got to watch me transform physically and spiritually, but more than that, they got to experience practical love from real life SUPERHEROES, namely our friends, my PBAU students,

PBAU coworkers, people from my past and total strangers who made it their priority to take care of them. Shanel and Daniel got their own testimony of faith in action and that is something I could have never envisioned would happen as a result of the cancer journey.

Two significant events come to mind as I recall the ways in which God took care of us and allowed the children to see with their own eyes. Before I was admitted to the hospital for the long transplant journey, someone came to our home with a generous financial donation. It was a gift sent from the person's loved one who was impacted by a public speaking presentation I delivered years ago. Secondly, an organization was informed about my cancer journey through one of their members. They collected funds and delivered it to my home in time for Christmas to make sure my children would not have to do without a good Christmas because I had been hospitalized and unemployed for a significant part of the year. Even though the children lived with the fear of watching me battle the disease and the possibility that I could die, they were also able to grow their faith because of the many times God blessed us miraculously and took care of our practical needs.

When I was home, the children could share with me according to their comfort level. As treatment progressed and I was able to give and receive hugs from family, I made sure Shanel and Daniel knew that I was still the affectionate, accessible mommy they knew, and I freely hugged as often as I was able to. Even when it was difficult to prepare meals due to fatigue, I still tried to do what I could to show them that I was still their caring, attentive mother. Children still need some semblance of normalcy so that they will understand that just because the routines have been disrupted, the quality and consistency of care remains intact.

One of the most significant blessings we received was the support and sacrifices made by my mother who took her grandmother ministry to the next level. My mother frequently traveled several hours to be with the children while I was in the hospital to make sure they were cared for in my absence. She was one of the safest, most solid, secure people who was there for the children. One of the most touching, tender memories that I have of her tender, loving care occurred during hurricane Irma as I lay in the hospital. I could not be at home with the children, but Mommy was. She described having both kids lay with her in my bed when the electricity was gone as they listened to the raging winds and rain. Both kids snuggled in closer as they listened in terror to the turmoil taking place outside. Knowing that my mother was there to provide the emotional, social and spiritual support was one of the best blessings we could have received during those months.

The cancer journey also revealed other people (**_SHE_**ROES) who were deemed to be solid, sensitive, sincere and safe for the children to share and interact with. It was bad enough that they had to live with the constant fear that perhaps their mother might die because of the disease. Consequently, it was crucial that they had the right kind of people with whom they could share these and other fears. Children are smart enough to know when adults are too timid to tell the truth. They know when people are being evasive to avoid talking about uncomfortable subject matters. My kids knew when relatives and church folks were over-emphasizing the spiritual component in order to minimize the real possibilities. It is not that they didn't have faith, but they knew that cancer took their Grandfather Eric Lewis, and had legitimate reason to wonder if it would take their Mommy, too. A significant blessing was the people who came alongside to help the children process their feelings while they were going through the journey. Not every adult is emotionally equipped to have age-appropriate conversations with children regarding major life changes. Some people choose to over-spiritualize things (particularly Christians), while others avoid all discussion with the children as though it is best to ignore what is happening. Neither approach is ideal because it insults children's awareness and intelligence. Acting as though a sickness or a major life change is not occurring sends a message to children that their instinct, intuition, feelings and fears are not valid.

Thankfully, God had already placed professional, licensed counselors and youth leaders in their lives with whom they already had a relationship. These **SHEROES** ('adopted' aunts and mentors) knew the importance of providing a safe space for the children to speak about what was happening without having to bottle up all their feelings. This outlet facilitated temporary times of relief when they could let off steam, ask questions, cry and just be kids. These people were emotionally, socially and spiritually equipped to help the children navigate those awkward, but necessary, conversations. Through intentional interaction, my sister-friends provided an outlet and created opportunities for the children to share when they needed to. I applaud my closest friends who not only created avenues for me to share candidly when I needed to, but provided a sacred space for my children to do so as well. We will forever be grateful to these godly, strong, wise women–Dr. Andrea Cunard, Pastor Sandra Valentine, Lisa Hoang, Amelia Gillis, Zaneen Thompson, Latosha Cherry, LaRue Howard and Lorene Pinnock provided a safe space for me and my children.

The best part of having my children go through the process was that they got to see the grandeur of God's goodness displayed through the practical demonstrations of love from people. Having cancer and undergoing regular in-hospital treatment meant I could not go to work or even do work from home. Being unemployed posed several challenges because I was not wealthy or in a financial position to live comfortably without consistent income. As I write this two years later, it is amazing to see how my financial life is still impacted by the loss of gainful employment, regular paychecks and employer insurance benefits; however, from the very beginning of the journey, God assured me that He would take care of every need. **"I'm your Father and I will always take care of you. Watch Me take care of you!!"** He promised as I relinquished my concerns in prayer and praise. I did not know how He was going to take care of the new expenses incurred by dealing with a cancer diagnosis, and I certainly did not know how the rent and other financial obligations were going to be handled. But the Lord always reminded me that although I had a small family who had the mind but not the means, He had people assigned to take care of the various needs. **Until one's life changes drastically and regular earnings cease, people have no idea what it is like when one must rely on aid to live and take care of the obligations. The job you're currently doing may not be exactly what you want it to be, but until things change, make the very best of it and be grateful.**

Looking back, I can understand that people did not readily recognize our financial needs because as a distinguished lady and mother, I always chose to put the best image forward and not greet the world with dowdiness. Many had no way of knowing that it took great creativity to make ends meet and finance the other essential expenses that occurred from time to time. Consequently, I am grateful for the people who saw beneath the smiles, nice outfits and overall appearance and chose to bless us with food, clothes and special treats. I appreciate the ones who realized that the financial challenges did not automatically end when I was declared cancer free in August 2017, because I was still unemployed for two more years. Without me asking, people blessed us with nice clothing, fancy accessories (because they knew I was still a glamorous girly girl) and other things that people don't usually think about when one is without gainful employment. God was true to His words when He said there were people assigned to take care of me. To this day as I write this, **I am constantly in awe of the ones who choose to listen and immediately obey when the Lord and their kind heart prompts them to do something for me and my family.** I was surprised and shocked to realize that the ones who I thought would rally around us and rise to the occasion usually weren't the ones who showed up with tangible blessings. Instead, it has always been the ones who God knew could be trusted to be His hands and heart extended.

One of my favorite hymns written by Southern Gospel song writer, Vesphew Ellis says, "Oh to be His hands extended, reaching out to the oppressed. Let me touch Him, let me touch Jesus, so that others may know and be blessed" (Ellis, 1964). The words of this song came to life in our lives as people from near and far chose to be God's hands and heart extended. My mother, Joyce Wallace and stepfather, Clement Wallace, frequently traveled from South Florida to stay at the hospital with me and at home with the children. My sister, Alecia Lewis, frequently left work to spend the night with me in the hospital or at home with the kids. My brother, Othniel Lewis, regularly traveled from Jamaica to be with us as well. Other relatives and close friends traveled to be with us and help lighten the load. They made many major sacrifices to stand with us through it all, and for that we will always be grateful. My small family reflected selfless love, service, support and sacrifice.

In addition, my university students, coworkers, and community colleagues showed up for us in thoughtful ways. My River of Life Christian Center church leaders and family looked out for us and blessed us with so much more than prayers. The head deacon at church called regularly and I was assigned my own deaconess to check in with me and update the church leaders of my progress on a regular basis. It was a special day when my pastor Marvin Jackson and his wife Deborah Jackson, spent time with me in the hospital on his birthday. River of Life Christian Center church members took the children shopping for their favorite fast food and clothes. A few dedicated River of Life church sisters coordinated my transportation to medical appointments and hospital admissions. Cathy Farmer-Kindell, Marcia Miller and Reshon Moore were the three regular drivers who provided the blessing of transportation to the essential appointments and admissions. Later in the recovery journey, I was even blessed with friends who left their homes and livelihood in Jamaica and put their own lives on pause to stay with me and take care of me for weeks so that Mom could resume her work schedule in South Florida. Dawn Martin and Dotlyn Facey are the two **SHEroes** who left their homes in Jamaica to take turns caring for me. High school friends, childhood peers, and people who were impacted by my parents' ministry rallied around us with visits, phone calls, messages and tangible blessings. Even strangers rose to the occasion to make sure that needs were met, bills were paid, and those initial medical expenses were taken care of. My children and I got to see, feel and experience the goodness of God during the cancer journey (and we still do).

Perhaps if the cancer diagnosis never happened, we would not have known how much we were loved, cared for and supported. Personally, I never knew that I was loved by so many. People say "love you" so casually that it sometimes sounds like a cliché that we hear with our ears but not necessarily in our hearts. It took a cancer journey to show my children and I that we were certainly loved, and that God was truly for us and standing with us. My children have memories and experiences from those years that no one can take away or duplicate. They saw with their own eyes the creative and consistent provision of God in ways that amazed them. Although cancer added to other things they were dealing with, it was another way for them to experience trauma and live through it. Shanel and Daniel learned first-hand that "life happens" but we must go through it and grow from it. They became even more resilient and tenacious (and Lord knows, they were already troopers).

Only time will tell how the stress of watching their mother deal with cancer prepared them for tough times and challenging circumstances. It is my hope, belief and earnest prayer that their lives will be better, more purposeful and significant because at an early age, they walked through the cancer journey with their mom. Years later (as I reflect and write this), we are surveying the landscape, evaluating the debris, assessing the damage and using appropriate measures to deal with the aftermath. We went through a storm and now we process the ways in which our outlook, perspectives and entire lives have changed. I came out as a cancer survivor and my children emerged as co-survivors.

Shannan's Heroes

Joyce & Clement Wallace (Mom and Dad)
Alecia Lewis (aka Allie)
Othniel Lewis (aka Otty)
Zaneen Thompson, and her sons Michael & Andre
Dr. Andrea & Justin Cunard
Lisa Hoang
Sandra Valentine
LaRue Howard
Bishop Leslie & Lorene Pinnock
Latosha Cherry
Cathy Farmer-Kindell
Reshon Moore
Marcia Miller
Amelia Gillis
Brenda Lewis and her sons Kevin & Shawn
Dawn Martin
Dotlyn Facey

Perspective Facebook Posts–Insights Inspired by Challenging Times

May 12, 2017, 11:15 PM

#GIFTOFPRESENCE–My Princess, firstborn, mini-me Shanel (Nelly Blair) blew me away yesterday with her 'Countdown to Mother's Day' love letters. The last few days, she hid a letter so I could 'discover' it. But when it became clear that we were going to have to call 911, she went for the others, placed them all in an envelope and sent them to the hospital with me. WOW WOW!!!!! In her own thoughtful way, she gave me more than company, she gave me presence that transcends distance. I can read those letters and feel her heart even though I am not next to her at home. My daughter knows my number one love language and speaks it fluently and eloquently. We will love on each other and 'turn up' in this hospital room on Mother's Day. I am honored to be her mother!

Aug 6, 2017, 9:38 AM

There are 2 things that are dangerous for a cancer patient–stress and fever (I had both last night). So you can imagine my joy when twice last night I woke up to see my son standing over me praying. My kids are troopers who are dealing with a lot but they make me proud to see their commitment to the things of God. Recently while having her devotion, Shanel came to my room to get a communion cup to include in her time of worship. Please pray for them that God will guard their hearts, honor their efforts and cover them in all things. Nelly Blair and DJ are my medicine, my motivation and my reason for striving to be a true Christian in my attitudes and actions.

Aug 26, 2017, 11:37 AM

You know what I've realized more and more in this season?? TREAT PEOPLE RIGHT BECAUSE YOU NEVER KNOW WHO WILL SHOW UP FOR YOU WHEN YOU NEED THEM TO. Not all testimonies are meant to be shared but take it from me, if you treat people right, THE RIGHT PEOPLE will be there when LIFE HAPPENS. Trust me, if you keep on living, life is going to happen to you, something's coming your way and you shall reap the treatment you sowed into other people's lives. #ChooseKindness #PeopleBeforeThings #LetThingsGo #ChooseTheHigherRoad #FamilyFirst #TodayCouldBeYourLast #WordsToTheWise

Sept 26, 2017, 8:00 PM

"People get upset with you when you no longer fit into the dress they bought for you. But the dress does not fit anymore"– Overheard my son give this perspective to his sister as they discussed a matter together. WOW, his analogy perfectly describes people's reaction when they refuse to accept that your season has changed and you no longer fit where you were before. #WisdomOfAChild #KidsAreSoPerceptive

CHAPTER 16

Impact on the Caregivers

When a loved one is diagnosed with cancer, the ones who choose to journey alongside and provide appropriate care are heroes. I deliberately used the word "choose" because not every spouse, parent, sibling, relative, or friend automatically makes the decision to be there for their loved one in the cancer journey. In most cases, those who make that choice do so because of proximity, deep love, compassion and kindness. They are usually the ones who can tolerate the rough, raw realities, process frightening information and hold their emotions in check in order to provide physical, emotional, spiritual and financial assistance. Needless to say, their emotions are greatly impacted because of the access given. Being able to watch the patient's body succumb to the sickness and effects of treatment is very stressful for caregivers. Most of the time they feel helpless because they don't know what to say or do in order to alleviate the person's pain, discomfort or despair, but they become heroes in the cancer journey because they give the best of themselves – the gift of presence.

Like the patient, caregivers also live with a heightened aware-ness that death could be inevitable which means they have to compartmentalize their own emotions in order to protect their sick loved one. The patient undergoes the physical and emotional trauma of the disease, but the caregiver experiences a myriad of emotions which range across the spectrum, including fear, anger, worry, sadness and guilt. Some question why their loved one got sick and not them, especially if the patient is a young child. They operate from a place of impotence and in some cases, hopeless-ness. It is frightening to watch the various changes and annoying side effects that seemingly become the norm for the patient. As a result, caregivers are forced to summon daily strength, courage and bravery to observe these things and still maintain an attitude of hope, faith, kindness and optimism. In some cases, in order to balance their feelings, frustrations and fears, caregivers may come across as overly controlling or overcompensating. Not being sure of how to process their own emotions may cause them to treat the patient with excessive care, but it is all from a place of love and concern. The wonderful thing is that when a cancer patient becomes a survivor, the caregivers are considered co-survivors.

One of the most touching and tender Facebook posts that my sister made was the following. As you read it, you will understand why it is one of my favorites.

June 12, 2017 at 7:56 PM

Alecia Lewis wrote:

"We will ride the storm together"

Last year as Hurricane Matthew geared up to wreak havoc on Florida, my sister and I found ourselves in a peculiar situation, forced to endure the storm by ourselves, as various factors led to us being by ourselves during the time the storm was to hit. My sister called me and made it clear, she's coming over, and we will ride the storm together.

Many storms have struck us since then. The cancer diagnosis was like bolts of lightning to our system...we never saw it coming! Like Hurricane Matthew, the threat of disaster forced us to brace for impact. Our sisterhood has become stronger. Growing up, we weren't always close, as sibling rivalry often brought a wedge between us. Yet, today, like so many days recently, we ride the storm together. I've been so encouraged and inspired by her tenacity. I've tried to be there for her as best as I know how. I spend many nights at the hospital when she's there, so we can ride the storm together. I just want to be there for her.

Last weekend something amazing happened, after Chemotherapy, she had a strong urge to be with me. She needed to be with her sister. I was all too happy to be there for her and as I prepped the room for her arrival, sanitized everything and made sure she would have what she needed, I became happy at the thought that I could be there for her. Interesting however, was the turnaround. I thought she was here so I could be THERE FOR HER, instead, she was here so SHE could be THERE FOR ME!

She was weak when she emerged out of bed early Saturday morning, but she said to me, "come let us pray." I listened as she prayed...for ME! Sunday, even lower in energy, she lay in bed and worshipped and encouraged me. Today, I left work early and got home to the sounds of worship filling the house. She was too tired to stay up but she sat in bed, set worship music on and let the atmosphere be filled with peace. She has been worshipping on my behalf. Praising on my behalf. Declaring faith on my behalf, as if she detected I could use a little help. Sometimes it gets to be too much to bear. So as I was beginning to have the physical impacts of the emotional turmoils (over the past ten months), she gave the ultimate gift of #presence! Her presence, despite her pain, was a gift to me. Plus she helped usher in the presence of God, which is far better than any other remedy.

Shannan, I love you! You are indeed a gift. I PRAY God will completely heal and restore you. For what it's worth, this has been the best thing I've received in a long time. The gift of presence! Thank you!

CHAPTER 17

Impact on Couples: Sex, Side Effects & Satisfaction

Recently, I had an amusing and eye-opening conversation about sex after cancer with someone very close to me. It made me realize that some people wonder if a cancer patient/survivor can be sexually active during and after the journey. I can't share from personal experience because I have been celibate by choice for several years. However, I can address this important subject as one who still has sexual urges, appreciate my sensuality and desire wholeheartedly to be sexually active again (or as I said to the person, "God is not going to take me Home and not have me experience and enjoy sex again before that happens."). Good Reads website (2020) quotes Woody Allen as saying, "Sex is the most fun you can have without laughing." This is certainly true as it represents an essential need that God gave us. We were designed to have sex for procreation and pleasure. As I described and encouraged years ago in a Facebook post, "Sex is such a gift;

package nicely, open discreetly, share regularly." Most adults would agree that life without sex is not the ideal, unless that is one's choice. It is an important part of our human expression and experience and should be treated as such.

Being diagnosed with cancer and undergoing various testing and treatment will often mean that people may not feel the desire for sexual activity because the body is in fighting and survival mode. The physical and psychological changes affect sexual desire and the ability to engage in sexual activities. But it does not mean sexual feelings totally go away. In the first few months of treatment, I still had thoughts and desires for sex, which was an indication that I was still functioning like a normal human being. Once chemotherapy started, the doctors gave me medication to put my body in early menopause and I was totally ok with that. "Goodbye monthly periods," I thought, and as far as fertility goes, I informed them that I was perfectly ok with the possibility that chemotherapy would prevent me from having more children. I already had my two gifts from God and had no desire to conceive again (unless God had other plans in the next season of my life). It was reassuring whenever I felt any indication that my hormones were still behaving as usual. However, as treatment progressed, I could tell that my libido was also being impacted because I had no desire for anything sexual. In my case, that was irrelevant because as I previously indicated, I was not sexually active at the time and had no desire to be for a while. But it made me wonder, what do couples do who are in a committed relationship? What happens to a couple when a cancer diagnosis is given? How does a couple live out the "through sickness and in health" part of the marriage vows? How does cancer treatment disrupt flirtation and sexual routines in a relationship? Well, I couldn't answer those questions from personal experience, but I thought of two couples who beautifully and boldly demonstrated how to love well and keep the fire burning even during a cancer journey.

I reflected on my own parents who willingly, consistently and lovingly demonstrated what it means to stick together "for better or worse, through sickness and in health, till death do us part". As a 16-year-old, I had to watch cancer invade our family's life, disrupt our routines, reveal people's hearts and observe real Christlike love on full display. One morning as I watched my father shaving, I noticed a bump on the side of his neck. "Daddy, what is that?" I asked with curiosity and concern. I don't recall his response at that moment, but he later went to the doctor who said he had an infection, prescribed antibiotics and sent him home. Fast forward a few weeks or months later, he had to get a biopsy to determine why his neck was swelling. Dad was diagnosed with non-Hodgkin's lymphoma. A kind pastor who lived in Fort Lauderdale encouraged him to travel from Jamaica to seek treatment in Florida, and just like that, our lives were disrupted by this devastating diagnosis. Mommy took an unpaid leave of absence from her job to travel with my father to become his full-time caregiver. This change in our family dynamic meant we had to be cared for by close friends of the family because we were young, school-aged children. (Incidentally, Dotlyn Facey was one of the persons who stayed at our home while our parents were in America. Fast forward to 27 years later, and she was in my home once again taking care of me as the patient.)

Each time we traveled to Fort Lauderdale to see our parents, I marveled at Mommy's strength and commitment to the man she loved. I saw firsthand what it looked like to love someone through sickness. No one could have predicted that Daddy was going to get sick because he rarely had a cold, a stomachache or anything remotely close to illness. I saw the way Dad still looked at Mommy and knew if he could dance with her as usual, he would. They were lovers in the real sense of the word, and I will always be grateful for the way they loved purely, passionately and purposefully.

Upon his return to Jamaica after treatment, we had many opportunities to hear his heart as he provided instruction and direction to each of us. At the time, we had no idea that these would be our last weeks together as a family with Daddy. In December 1990, he gave us money to buy Mommy's birthday gift (always the planner and provider). Four days after Mommy's birthday, he transitioned to his heavenly Home and I am sure he went there carried on the wings of love and consistent Christlike care from the woman he loved all his life.

As I went through my cancer journey, I grew to love and admire a couple who was also going through theirs. I had (and still have) the honor of observing Pastors Lace and Arthur Taylor as they boldly and beautifully battle her cancer diagnosis. I met Lace Taylor many years ago as we attended the same church. Years later, she and Arthur launched Overcomers Ministry in Orlando. When I found out that she was battling cancer, my heart broke because it seemed like cancer had no right to invade her body. But when I was diagnosed in 2017, Lace became a point of ref-erence and an example of how to go through the process as a faith-filled Christian woman. Most Christians that I knew of who dealt with cancer chose to do it silently and privately, so I had not seen a person publicly go through their cancer journey and use it to minister to others. I didn't even know it could be done. When the Lord prompted me to share as I went through my journey, I thought about Lace and was inspired that if she could do it, so could I. I admired her willingness to share, pray and display grace under pressure. I appreciated her advice, support and candid con-versations because both of us were a part of an exclusive club we didn't sign up to join. We shared chemo cancer complaints, laughed about the various similarities and prayed for each other in a way that others could not. We spoke the language of cancer and although we would not have wanted it that way, we both accepted that it was a part of our journey and determined to make God proud by the way we went through the process.

Like me, Lace had no idea that cancer had invaded her body because she was busy with life, singing and ministering as usual. In the spring of 2015, she was preparing to host a women's conference in Chicago but had committed to donating blood at a Blood Drive. However, after she made the deposit, the nurse became alarmed because her blood count was extremely low. She was immediately sent to the hospital to receive a blood transfusion because her body was down to one and a half pints of blood. Medical News Today (Sissons, 2020) states that "an average adult has between 9 and 12 pints of blood in their body" which means she had anemia caused by blood loss. Several tests only made matters worse because nothing revealed where the blood was going in her body. Weeks later, Lace and her husband received the devastating diagnosis that she had stage 3 colorectal cancer.

Picture it–As Pastor Arthur sat stunned and numb, with his arms folded around his waist, Lace reacted to the group of doctors who had delivered the news. "You all need to take that _____ and get the _____ out. You've got the wrong girl!!!" With a look of surprise and embarrassment, Arthur tried to give the appropriate "calm down Babe"' look, but Lace gave him the hand (more like the unmistaken upright palm that meant "don't even say another word!") and yelled, "No, I don't have to take all this in. Tell them to leave the room now!!!!" Arthur described the feeling of impotence as he realized how powerless he was to do or say anything. Eventually he had to pull himself together to go home and gather the essential items she would need as the reality of extended hospitalization stared him in the face.

Left alone with her thoughts, feelings and raw emotions, Lace ignored the pain in her body and began to say the name of Jesus. All the years of singing, teaching, and preaching did not prepare her for the despair and disappointment that she felt. There were no words that made sense of what she was told as the explanation for the symptoms she was having. For weeks, she had been feeling intense pain in her belly, neck and throat. At first, she thought it could be female related issues, but the pain escalated. Not wanting to bother her husband, she suffered in silence, choosing to "tough it out" until the night she had to tell him what she was feeling, but never in her life did she expect that the symptoms were attributed to cancer.

As the protector, provider and priest of his home, Arthur found himself devoid of answers because he had no way of thinking that God would allow them to add to their already difficult life. Years before they had to bury their young son and more recently, they were dealing with major financial hardship which meant that they were used to ministering to others but going home with no electricity or basic needs in the home. He recalled that when he went home to pack Lace's clothes for the hospital stay, all he could think of was the reassuring words God gave him when his son died. Somehow those memories gave him the strength that God would be with him in this new challenge as well. Moreover, he knew that his attitude and approach would be one of unending commitment to his wife because that was what he promised her 33 years ago. Although he was afraid that he would not be strong enough for her and that there was nothing he could do to change the diagnosis, he promised God that his approach would not change towards her now that she was stricken with a cancer diagnosis. Arthur stated that 3 months before he and Lace got married, they talked about their individual definition of love and their views on marriage as a covenant, which they both agreed meant unconditional love till death with no option for departure or divorce from each other. These sentiments were also shared with the pastor who gave them premarital counseling. Their pastor endorsed Arthur to Lace's parents with these words, "He doesn't have a giving up spirit. He will endure fights and not quit. He is inspired to be a family man and caretaker because he never had one around." These same commitments led Arthur to love his wife unconditionally as she went through (and to this date is still undergoing) cancer treatment.

Their sex life was impacted because of the type of cancer, treatment plans and side effects. However, that didn't prevent them from being intimate with each other as they chose to find creative ways to express intimacy. They both indicated that they acknowledged when they were in the mood ("Are you horny, because I am horny right now"). Both Lace and Arthur explained that couples in love know that sexual satisfaction is not always the result of sexual intercourse but taking time to touch, talk, laugh and do things together regularly. There were times when the inability to perform took a toll on Lace and she struggled to not be hard on herself, but being a sensitive, caring husband meant that Arthur knew when and how to console, comfort, reassure and reaffirm her. A woman's self-image can be significantly affected during a cancer journey because she looks and feels different. Even if a woman does not articulate those feelings, every one of us wants to feel and be seen as desirable, sexy, appealing, useful and beautiful. I'm sure the same is true for men. It takes a mature, understanding, loving, sensitive partner to recognize their partner's need for affirmation, admiration, attention, appreciation and affection. It takes a strong, selfless, sincere spouse to see beyond their own needs for regular sexual release and show their partner that their love and passion is not held hostage to the next orgasm. It takes will-power and integrity to stay faithful when one's partner is not able to perform certain sexual acts due to sickness, side effects, or surgery complications.

One must be prepared for the physical, physiological and psychological impacts that cancer and treatment could possibly have on one's sex life, but the reality is that not everyone will be affected in these ways. Whether you are single or in a sexual relationship when cancer hits the body, the sickness and treatment will disrupt regular sexual routines. It is best to discuss sexual matters (preferences, positions, permissions) with health care providers so that appropriate actions can be taken during and after the cancer journey. Sex is possible during chemotherapy treatment, but partners must be careful because:

> Chemotherapy can be excreted in vaginal secretions for 48-72 hours after a treatment. You should use a condom for oral sex or intercourse during this period to prevent your partner from being exposed to the chemotherapy. (This includes IV and oral chemotherapy.) (OncoLink.org, 2018).

Men and women have similar responses and side effects as it pertains to sex during and after cancer. The OncoLink website indicates the following:

> ***Some men experience a loss of desire for sex, an inability to achieve or maintain an erection, inability to reach orgasm or have a change in orgasm (duration, intensity or dry ejaculation), experience pain during sex or just do not find sex pleasurable.***

Only time will tell which of these responses will affect a man dealing with cancer. The same is true for women because each person responds differently. However, *"Some women experience a loss of desire for sex, an inability to have an orgasm, experience pain during sex or just do not find sex pleasurable."*
According to the OncoLink Team on the website OncoLink.org:

> *There are a few factors that determine if sexual activity is safe during treatment.*
>
> *In general, sexual activity is fine during treatment as interest, energy and comfort levels allow. Women may not feel up to sexual intimacy after surgeries or during chemo and radiation. Hugging, holding hands and massages may feel good and be comforting.*
>
> *If you had surgery involving the pelvic area (gynecologic cancers, colorectal and anal cancers), you may need to allow extra time for healing before having sex that involves vaginal or rectal penetration (with penis, fingers, toys, vibrators or dilators). If you are being treated for an oral cancer, use caution during oral sex.*
>
> *If you have a low white blood cell count or low platelet count (concern arises with platelets below 50,000), you will need to refrain from any sexual activity that involves vaginal or anal penetration. This is because there is an increased risk of infection or bleeding when your counts are low.*

There are certain chemotherapies that caution you about becoming pregnant while on treatment and for a specific amount of time after treatment is done. See the package insert for your chemotherapy or ask your pharmacist for this information.

In my humble opinion, I believe that the most important thing to remember is that honest communication with oneself, one's partner and healthcare providers is necessary to navigate sex during and after cancer. Just because this diagnosis had the audacity to disrupt one's life, it does not necessarily have to decimate one's ability to enjoy intimacy and sexual pleasure, especially long-term. It begins with recognizing the way one feels physically and emotionally and expressing those feelings (or lack thereof). Be honest about feelings of self-consciousness, insecurity, changes in body image and anything that is different in one's outlook about sexual activities. Ask specific questions to get realistic answers. Make no assumptions about anything for fear of how one could come across. Pace yourself and be willing to make realistic adjustments, especially initially for the sake of comfort. When the feelings emerge, give yourself permission to make out like horny teenagers who risk getting caught, even if that is massaging, fondling and checking to see how one's body will respond to touch, tasting and teasing. Flirt and seduce once those feelings emerge; go with the flow and be creative. If feasible and affordable, you may even have to get a new bed if the one used during treatment triggers memories of the diagnosis and the many days spent in recovery. Use doctor approved products to lubricate if necessary and seek a prescription designed to help with vaginal dryness and increased blood flow to the penis. Find new ways to achieve orgasms but don't set out with that as the end goal. Recognize that your body and brain are working overtime to repair you, so be patient with the process. Don't give up on your sex life completely just because you're in a temporary state of being renewed. If you are lucky and blessed to have a partner who knows how to love in actions and attitudes, which comes from a place of care, consideration, compassion and unconditional love, you will be able to have the kind of sex life that works for both of you. Seek satisfaction in new and creative ways to ensure that your sex life and sensuality are not discarded.

CHAPTER 18

Remission and Recovery

O n the morning of August 17, 2017, I was given the great news that there was no more leukemia in my system. Earlier in the week, I did a bone marrow biopsy surgery which revealed that no cancer was detected, and I could now move forward with preparations for the transplant. Prior to that surgery, the doctors frequently commented that they were pleased with the way my body responded to and tolerated the strong chemotherapy that was administered. This was necessary to get my body to the point where the cancer cells would be eliminated in order to move forward with the next essential part of the treatment plan. In order to cure the leukemia and extend my life, the plan was for me to get a bone marrow transplant and thankfully for me, my very own sister, Alecia Lewis, was my donor.

I learned through those months that healing is a process which is often lengthy. It takes time and patience to heal well. When we are used to operating at a certain level and handling a variety of things, it is very difficult to slow down, pace ourselves and allow healing to take place. Going through the cancer journey reiterated the importance of patience, self-love and discipline to ensure adequate rest, proper healing and a successful recovery.

"Sit still and heal" is a powerful instruction that became a significant part of my recovery process because it was used in a sermon preached by my pastor, Dr. Marvin Jackson. In the latter part of 2015, I changed churches as an act of obedience to God. People who are not followers of the Lord may not understand this, so let me put it in context. In the spring and summer months of 2015 I became agitated in my spirit sensing that a shift was going to take place but had no idea what that was. At the time, there were three significant matters that caused me to pray earnestly for direction, so I had a Post-It note on my work desk with these prayer requests – my job at PBAU, my house situation and my church involvement. I wanted the Lord to provide clear direction regarding each one because it was important that I remained in His perfect will.

At 12:26 a.m. on July 12, 2015, I heard the Lord give me the first answer regarding my list. It was my birthday and I began the day worshiping and reading the Word. He led me to Isaiah 52 in the Message version of the Bible. The chapter heading was titled "GOD IS LEADING YOU OUT OF HERE." I read the chapter and began taking notes as my spirit immediately knew it was time for me to leave my place of worship. I had no idea why I had to leave the church at that time or where I was supposed to go, but I knew beyond the shadow of a doubt that I had to step out in faith and obedience. I visited several churches and enjoyed the various styles of worship, but when I was led to the River of Life Christian Center, I knew that this was the place where Father God wanted me to be. At first, I didn't understand why the Lord led me to that church because in some ways, it was different from what I was used to in my previous church experiences. Granted, I was used to Pastor Marvin Jackson's teaching style of sermons because for many years, I watched his television program before going to work every morning. I never really envisioned attending that church though – to me, it was not what I was used to. However, after attending a few services, I knew that I was in my "set place" with the right people and the right spiritual covering. I will forever be grateful that God gave me clear direction on my birthday in July 2015. After several weeks of fasting and prayer (in addition to receiving many confirmations), I wrote the church leadership regarding my decision to leave, handed over to the designated worship leader replacement, then left after fulfilling my final obligation in that organization.

Years later, it is now abundantly clear that the Lord gave me that instruction to change churches in 2015. God knew all that was about to happen in my personal, professional and physical life, especially the cancer diagnosis. He wanted to make sure that I was repositioned and replanted in the right environment where my solid, sincere support system would be. I didn't have to ask my River of Life family members for assistance because they eagerly, willingly, consistently and lovingly offered the gifts of their time and treasure. The River of Life Christian Center is where I was supposed to receive the best care for what my family and I needed, so when God said, "It's time to leave," He knew why. He knew everything that was about to happen in the story of my life, and He made sure I was already in the right place with the right people.

A few months after I joined the River of Life, Pastor Jackson referred to the story in the Bible in which grown men had to be circumcised. Before they could resume normal activity and get into battle, they were cautioned to "sit still and heal". That message resonated in my mind and spirit because I needed to wait a while before joining the choir and volunteering in other areas of the ministry. I had to give myself permission to grieve the loss of people and things (tangible and intangible). I needed to heal the parts of my heart that were broken and filled with disappointment. For years I was a worship and arts leader who gave everything in ministry, but in this new season at the River of Life, I needed to take an extended break from public service and rest from all the years of frequent singing, planning, coordinating, meetings, rehearsing and leading. I needed to rest and rejuvenate my body, mind, soul and spirit. I needed to be poured into instead of always being the one pouring into others. "Sit still and heal" meant that while I took a break from serving publicly, I would receive healing through the Word of God taught by a pastor who seemed to be speaking directly to all my situations at the time. It meant being healed through the praise and worship as each song and the worship leader's ad lib comments seemingly went right through to the hurting areas of my heart. I received healing from kind, loving and embracing people who didn't know who I was, but freely poured in compassion, care and Christlike love. I took several months before I was ready to join the choir and connect in other areas of the ministry. Looking back, I am so glad that I heeded Pastor Jackson's words and patiently waited to resume public service in ministry.

Needless to say, "sit still and heal" played a significant role in my cancer journey because I adapted this same approach to recovery. Even though it was frustrating, restricting, and limiting, I had to heed those wise words to allow myself adequate time to heal even though it meant extended periods of isolation and restrictions. Many times, when a cancer patient succumbs to the sickness, it is not always the initial diagnosis that results in death, but it is infection, complication or other circumstances that occur during or after the process. Consequently, medical personnel provide strict instructions and warnings regarding rest, consistent care, and taking proper precautions to ensure healing.

If people choose to ignore the restrictions and rush the recovery process, there is a good chance that negative repercussions will be the result.

The same caution and warning can be applied to other areas of life that cause us to be wounded emotionally, mentally and physically. Too many times we experience major trauma and stressors that have an impact on the way we live our lives, yet we don't take the time to address and deal with those matters. We've been conditioned to toughen up and "keep it moving" because "life happens". So, we get "back to life, back to reality" without attending to the deep wounds in our heart, mind, soul and spirit.

This same principle applies in a spiritual context. When people experience spiritual wounds, stumble in their walk with the Lord or experience "church hurt", it is wise to take a moment to admit, address and allow time for healing. God certainly forgives and gives grace to deal with those painful situations, but we must also use wisdom to take a break and figure out what happened and how we need to move forward appropriately. Rushing back into full time service or ministry may not be the best thing to do. Spiritual wounds also deserve to be dealt with in practical ways, not only with a quick prayer.

ACTION ITEM

Ask yourself some intentional, probing questions that will help you discover what is hurting you and holding you back.

Please do yourself a BIG favor and answer the following questions:

What hurt you so deeply that you have never really recovered?

Who brought you so much pain that your outlook on relationships has changed?

What deliberate actions did you take to address those situations?

If you did nothing, why not?

What prevents you from taking ownership of your own healing?

What would healing look like to you?

What struggle (or sin) exists in your life that constantly causes you to stumble or make a mess of things?

Who has permission to hold you accountable and speak truth in love and kindness?

What steps can you take, starting now, to seek healing?

What are your thoughts on mental health?

Have you been to therapy or sought professional counseling to process your feelings?

If not, could your life, relationships and future benefit from seeking professional counsel?

Are you experiencing physical or physiological ailments that could be caused by unhealed issues?

You owe it to yourself, your loved ones, your past and your future to get the healing you deserve. Pain and heartache are a part of the life experience, but it doesn't have to define and debilitate all of it. Your healing is a choice – a deliberate decision to do what must be done to obtain it. Healing is a process so be kind to yourself and the person you are becoming by exercising patience, discipline and self-love. You are worth the time and the results that can be attained when you sit still and heal.

ACTION ITEM

Go to Shannan Lewis' Conquering Cancer Journey Channel to watch my YouTube video entitled, "Cancer Free as of 8.17.17"

**https://www.youtube.com/watch?v=L__
CeDpJsew&list=PLCGMdDzo2F3YOcvYF_
XEeMpjNerNTCs4d&index=12**

ACTION ITEM

Go to Shannan Lewis' Conquering Cancer Journey Channel to watch my YouTube video entitled, "Sit Still and Heal"

**https://www.youtube.com/watch?v=h-
PHWYOYOOVM&list=PLCGMdDzo2F3YOcvYF_
XEeMpjNerNTCs4d&index=23**

CHAPTER 19

Diary of a Cancer Patient

Shannan's Conquering Cancer Chronicles Shared Through Selected Facebook Posts

Jan 10, 2017, 9:30 PM–DIAGNOSIS DAY

On Sunday, I sang my heart out–"It's your breath in our lungs so we pour out our praise to you only...our hearts will cry, these bones will sing GREAT ARE YOU LORD". Still singing this, still reminding Him...

Jan 11, 2017, 11:51 AM

I can't get this song out of my head–"I must have the Savior with me, for I dare not walk alone. I must feel His presence near me and His arms around me thrown. Then my soul shall fear no ill. Let Him lead me where He will. I will go without a murmur and His footsteps follow still."

Jan 13, 2017, 5:26 PM

Soooooo, when I posted this on New Year's Eve, I had no idea how soon I would have to start with this CONQUERING process. I am more than a Conqueror through Christ Jesus. I am an overcomer, I am the righteousness of God in Christ Jesus. Every promise is yes and amen. God shall get His glory from every part of my story. #ThatsAllForNow

Jan 15, 2017, 8:18 PM

Pastoral ministry and leadership is more than what is done from the platform or the administrative offices. It is really about the impact they have with the ones in the pews and outside the walls. Pastor Deborah Jackson, LaRue Howard, Diaconates and the leadership of the River have loved on me like Jesus would. They call, they visit, they pray, they keep it real, and they connect with my family. I have church leaders who have me when it really matters!!!

Jan 16, 2017, 9:45 PM

It is amazing how one's life can change in ONE HOUR. We take too many things and people for granted. So listen up, do yourself a favor -

Stop holding grudges and carrying stale feelings for people
Stop internalizing pain—find a safe place to share
Stop telling lies to yourself and exaggerating things to others
Stop treating others with disdain—live life well
Stop eating after you are full, that is greedy
Stop staying up to watch the horrible late night news
Stop ignoring the people who are right there loving you
Stop warming the pews in churches—go change a life
Stop procrastinating and justifying bad behavior
Stop living outside of your means—stick with a budget
Stop stealing from God—worship with your tithes & offerings
Stop inviting toxic people into your life

Stop waiting for the right time to do the right things
Stop wasting emotional energy on things that mean squat
Stop putting off your medical checks—be wise
Stop beating yourself up—just make better choices
Stop withholding affection—love the ones you are with
Stop assuming you have tomorrow—it is not promised

Jan 19, 2017, 11:47 AM

What patient? I tell everyone that I meet that I am a guest in my penthouse suite, passing through as I undergo this process, so that God can get all kinds of glory. I am singing, worshiping, exhorting, encouraging and making sure they all get to see and hear about the Lord. Keep praying for me and my family as we trust God for miracles!!! Stand on His promises and when He tells you it's time for your testing, just submit to the process and walk out your faith. God's got this, God's got me!!! Shout out to my Diva Stylist Kat Jackson who came in and hooked me up. A girl's gotta stay pretty in all of this!!

Jan 22, 2017, 2:17 PM

As I prepare to drive by PBA on this my 2nd limo (ambulance) ride in two weeks, it no longer feels surreal. God has assigned me to walk this journey and has provided the GRACE I will need to get through victoriously to the other side. Just as my PBA journey began 10 years ago with many uncertainties, I have seen the hand of God walk me through the process to purpose. In the same way, I am committed to submitting to this new unfamiliar process so that God's purposes will be fulfilled. I know this will not be easy but I have a proven track record with the Lord so He will carry me, care for me, comfort me and give me the title of CONQUEROR!!! My Facebook friends and family, whatever He has assigned you to, receive the grace to walk through it. Know that it is always an integral part of your story for the sake of revealing Himself to you, others and magnifying the Kingdom. He is with me, He will be with us. May God's glory be revealed and His Name be glorified.

Jan 24, 2017, 6:49 AM

Well I wouldn't be true to this process if I only posted when I am in good spirits. THINGS JUST GOT REAL!!!! I feel different, weird, uncomfortable and tired. It takes extra energy to talk and although I like replying to the many messages, it is time to check them less. Nights are no longer for blissful sleep due to constant checks and treatments. My bathroom is my closest safe place. I am violated but feel no shame because my body must go through and be seen by all kinds of strangers. That being the case, this is NOT the ideal place for fun gatherings so I will have to limit guests. However, please continue to send prayers, kind wishes and a fierce expectation for a divine miracle (not the fake short lived kind). Although I look and feel different, I am still smiling between groans, setting the atmosphere with praise, and looking forward to the great life that will come after this. Thanks to my Palm Beach Atlantic University staff and students for coordinating care boxes for my children. God bless everyone has steps forward with the tangible, practical needs. Those acts of kindness are just as powerful to me like this treatment. Please cover my mommy Lady Joyce Wallace with prayers, encouragement and support. It's official—she is the assigned caregiver who will see and hear everything. Sigh...I am hungry but can't eat now because of my procedure scheduled for this morning. Life has changed now but my soul remains steadfast in THE ONE WHO IS WITH ME. Love and blessings to all who stand with me (in the past, in my present and in my amazing God-glorifying future). Until later...

Jan 25, 2017, 6:19 AM

So many things are coming AFTER THIS which will benefit the lives of many. But as I go through this experience, I also acknowledge the wonderful things that are happening even now before the "after this" phase. Relationships are being refined, reconnections have been made, people have stepped up to care in relevant tangible ways, love is being poured back into me from amazing places and people, lives are being inspired and encouraged, people are sharing their testimonies, God's love is being revealed in wonderful ways, people are hearing about who God is in spite of all that is happening. As you go through your "THIS", make sure you pay attention to all that is happening now instead of waiting for the after. Be mindful about your attitudes and actions knowing that in the midst of your "this" God can get all kinds of glory. "There will be glory after this, there will be victory after this, God's gonna turn it around, He will bring you out, there will be glory after this."

Jan 25, 2017, 2:20 PM
Shannan's first video after cancer diagnosis

SHANNAN'S THANKS

https://www.youtube.com/watch?v=bkxwgV4atPk&list=PLCG-MdDzo2F3YOcvYF_XEeMpjNerNTCs4d&index=2&t=0s

Jan 27, 2017, 5:01 PM

THE LEWIS FAMILY ARE BACK TOGETHER AGAIN–SPECIAL DAY IN MANY WAYS. FACING THIS FIGHT TOGETHER AGAIN. TRUSTING GOD TO DO WHAT ONLY HE CAN DO. #LewisLegacyLives #LoveThem #LastingLove

Jan 30, 2017, 5:30 AM

TRANSPARENT TESTIMONY TIME—As my nurse changed my new body buddy (the port), I reflected on the many things about myself and my life that has changed since January 10th. I have dropped 10 lbs, yesterday I could barely walk, I have learned to give myself injections, I am used to taking many medicines throughout the day, and I have a deeper appreciation for nurses and techs. But the biggest part of this journey so far is that GOD NEEDED TO PROVE TO ME AND OTHERS THAT HE'S GOT ME AND I AM LOVED FOR REAL. Last year I did not know for sure who loved me, liked me, who was looking out for me or being loyal to me. So much so, I had to make collages in my office to remind me of the people I felt were really there for me and truly cared. It was one of the toughest battles to no longer feel a sense of belonging, to feel like a reject, to have former friends step aside and go silent without even an "how are you?" Life required that I go through everything alone. I have always been used to pushing through and getting things done alone but that was different. I managed, I made it, in fact, I felt proud at the ways in which God gave me strategies to get through as an overcomer. I embraced the new season as a necessary wilderness that would propel me to pur-pose. Now that this part of the process has unfolded, I no longer feel alone, rejected or unloved. God needed to show me that He has many many people who have been assigned to love me well and to take care of the things that concern me. God needed to show me in a few short weeks that His resources surpass man's and nothing shall be withheld from me. God needed to remind me that He is my only true Source for all things (rent, medical bills, job security, friendship, care, covering, support and everything I will need). God needed to prove that His love for me is bigger and better than any other love there is and that He will be glorified as I bask in this season of love. #PushingThroughTheProcess #PraisingThroughPain

Feb 1, 2017, 8:42 AM
PUBLIC SERVICE ANNOUNCEMENT:

PEOPLE DON'T CAUSE OTHER PEOPLE TO GET CANCER, BAD CELLS CAUSE CANCER. THIS CAN BE TRIGGERED BY A COMBINATION OF FACTORS AND STRESSORS. NO ONE KNOWS WHEN THAT CAN HAPPEN. NO ONE SHOULD BLAME OTHERS FOR CAUSING SOMEONE'S CANCER. LET THERE BE NO SPECULATING, NO BLAMING, NO ACCUSING, NO FUSSING...GOD SAW THIS COMING AND HE ALLOWED IT SO PLEASE DO NOT LOOK FOR SOMEONE OR SOMETHING TO BLAME. THANK YOU!!!

Sincerely,

The Patient, the one going through this, the one trying to be strong for all of you, the one whose body this hit, the one who is trying to become a cancer survivor and testimony recipient

Feb 1, 2017, 8:30 PM
Joyce Wallace is hands down the best mother God could have picked out for me. All my life, especially after daddy died leaving her a young widow, I vowed to live a life that honors her. I always asked God to bless me so that I can bless her. So far, she is the one who has always been a blessing to me. I have many reasons to fight and beat this sickness, one of those reasons is for mommy. I have not gotten to the place in life where I can lavish her and love on her the way I want to. So long life, we have to do this because I plan to spoil my mother for all the love, sacrifices and support she has given to me.

Feb 3, 2017, 5:21 AM

Well, I'm up talking to Father about my latest concerns. I may as well share with those of you who are praying specific, strategic, prayers so you know where to direct your faith today.

1) My discharge is taking longer than anticipated due to insurance processing, pre-certs, etc. I am ready to go home and be an out-patient. I miss fresh air, cool breeze, traffic, I miss my home, my babies, my car, my life!!!!!!!!

2) I need a dining table to eat and work from (especially now that I will have to work from home). I moved last year but could not afford to get a table. My bed and coffee table will no longer work for meals and PBA work so I have to get one (Maybe you have an extra that is not being used, please inbox me a photo if you do)

3) I am losing weight rapidly and must go on a high calorie diet (doctor's orders). Although my goal was to lose weight this year, I did not expect it to happen this way and in a few short weeks. Pray that I stop losing weight

4) I need to safeguard whatever time I have on the books at work without losing all of it (sick, vacation, etc). FMLA may come into play but I am praying it does not get to that point

5) Preassigned people to be there at various parts of the journey so that mommy and my sister will not carry the bulk of this experience as caregivers (I am always concerned about caregivers because they need support too)

6) Pray for other people here who are having a harder time with their sickness, have no support system or worse, don't know the Lord

OK that's it for my morning prayers, thanks for joining me!!!

Feb 7, 2017, 8:23 AM

Hello, whaapen, how are you all doing? I needed to unplug to bask in the feelings of being home, sit in the reality of my new situation, silence the notifications and adjust to this new temporary normal (because total healing is coming and THIS won't be my reality forever). I needed to have temper tantrums with God (I am not always ok with what He has placed on me, so to keep our relationship real, I have to beat up on His chest sometimes—but He can handle it, If He could not, I would not serve Him or see Him as my Father, Friend, Faithful Companion). But the wonderful thing about being able to be honest with God is that He knows my heart and I don't need to impress Him by being spiritual all the time. I don't need to win Him over with superficial feelings. I can be real with every part of this (the concerns about my job and if I will have a job, the concerns about driving if I am so weak all the time, the concerns about people whose motives may be fuzzy, the concerns about hefty copayments, the concerns about side effects, the concerns about what the entire process will look like, the concerns about things I have no control over). I am glad I serve a God who gets all my concerns and validates each one. Whether I am singing a praise song or sighing with annoyance that this is my reality or shifting position to not feel my bone marrow biopsy spots, Father God gets it and He gets me, and He makes it ok to be who I am (all of me, just the way I am). People don't always give us the freedom to be who we are because people have unrealistic expectations about what we ought to be like as we go through life's experiences. Thankfully, Father God permits us to be real with ourselves and with Him. It is in these transparent, vulnerable and even the messy moments that we experience what is REAL about ourselves and our walk with the Lord. So, I am going to keep it real, up sometimes, down sometimes, big audacious faith sometimes and "what the heck are you doing to me" rants now and then. I am going to make Father proud that my faith is not confined to my church attendance but is alive and well even in the messy yucky annoying moments that I have to walk through. #KeepingItReal #MakingFatherProud

Feb 8, 2017, 5:17 AM

Road trip to Moffitt Cancer Center to meet the specialist. Little did the SISTERHOOD know that the next time we would meet for our ladies get together, it would involve taking me to my first specialist appointment. Don't wait until you need friends to make friends. Don't wait until something bad happens to reconnect with good friends. Don't poison the friendships you have over petty foolishness. Nurture the friendships God gave you. I am so grateful for genuine godly girlfriends (here with me and the ones who are far away but in my heart).

Feb 11, 2017, 2:31 PM

REST AND RECALIBRATE—Powerful reminder from my high school friend Suzie Sang. It confirmed what I have felt all day as my body is extra weak today. Getting up requires great effort and I am so tired, yet I realize how important rest is to the healing process. Why do we deprive ourselves much needed rest as if being busy and drained is a badge of honor? My dears, listen to your body and rest so you can regain, renew, recharge and recalibrate. My body is doing warfare as it cooperates with meds so I have to submit and rest. What does your body and mind need in order to function efficiently? Be wise and pause now and then. God never asked you to be a superhuman.

Feb 23, 2017, 7:01 AM

I miss singing and worshiping at church. This season has given me a new sympathy and sadness for the sick and shut-in who are not able to attend church. Now that I know what it feels like, I realize that when we have the chance to go to church, participate in the ministry and to support the vision of our leaders, we should. If I had known that this would have been my last time singing with my choir for a while, I would have given even more (not that I could have that night—see the facial expressions—LOL). Anyway, there are 2 points to this post:- DO NOT NEGLECT OR FORGET THE SICK AND SHUT IN CHURCH MEMBERS. Put a consistent plan in place to ensure they are kept in the loop, loved on regularly and receive regular church communications (my River leaders have stayed in touch with me and it feels great). Secondly, DO NOT TREAT YOUR CHURCH ATTENDANCE LIGHTLY because the time may come when you can no longer go even if you want to. And don't go to warm the pews, get involved, support the vision, give your all as unto the Lord. Don't get weary while doing good and remember it is an honor to serve. #LongingForMyChurchFamily #MissSingingOutLoud #LongToDanceForTheLord (photo credit:- Pastor Marvin A. Jackson)

Mar 2, 2017, 10:08 PM

I believe because you are the God of miracles (even though I did not want this way). As this chemo goes through my body and I try to prepare for what is about to happen, I am doing my best to not feel angry, alone, abandoned, or afraid. I am choosing to believe that God is indeed the God of wonders and eventually all of this will make sense. (Side note, I was in great spirits when I recorded this earlier today but tonight, I am not pleased. I am not ok...I am turning off my phone...I have to do this alone and this is real for me. But I wanted to share this Day 1 post because even if I am not pleased, I don't want to rob God of my praise moments).

Mar 3, 2017, 1:09 PM

We never really know what we are capable of handling until we are placed in certain situations. On Day 2 of Chemotherapy, I was able to join my hiring partners as we interviewed another applicant to work in my department (all from my bed with the treatment going in and sounding like my usual self). I never knew that I had it in me to multitask and still semi function but God knew. I never knew I could tolerate high doses of various treatments, nor that I would get used to having blood drawn all the time or that I could be somewhat ok with all this–BUT GOD KNEW WHAT HE HAS PLACED INSIDE OF ME AND WHAT I CAN HANDLE. That thing you are avoiding or think you can't handle may be your biggest shocker. You don't know what you are capable of dealing with and handling well, so don't back up, don't stay timid. Trust the process and your God to get you through. There is more in you and you can accomplish more than you realize. GO GET IT, GO MAKE IT HAPPEN, GO DISCOVER WHAT LIES BENEATH AND WHAT YOU CAN OVERCOME!!!!

Mar 13, 2017, 5:36 AM

Petty post:- It is 5:23 a.m. and I am yet to get undisturbed sleep. So much went wrong last night, I am hungry for real food, I am tired of this bed and all that comes with this confinement. I miss cooking, I hate not knowing what's coming next as this ridiculous sickness and treatment take over my days. I am not super anything and never asked for this. I am hungry and sleepy and questioning. I am bored and missing gainful employment. I feel stuck in somebody else's dream and I am not enjoying the nightmare. I can't exactly question or probe God for details or reasons but I have side eye this morning. Maybe because I long to cook in my own kitchen and eat like I used to, or perhaps it is because this is a draining, lonely, wearisome journey and I got the lead role. This is no warm and fuzzy, rally the troops to victory post. This is me being HUNGRY ANGRY TIRED AND SO OVER THIS!!!!!!!!

Mar 17, 2017, 8:13 PM

"When we expect God to show up and showoff in our situations, it is best not to speed up, shortchange or seek shortcuts. If we do, there is no telling what we will miss in the process or how many will miss their blessing because we want to hurry our process."–Shannan Cancer Conqueror in the making.

Mar 22, 2017, 9:58 AM

My FAITH in God allows me to trust His heart instead of twisting His hands to do what I want, when I want or how I want things to happen. That is not easy because the daughter in me wants to beg, plead, negotiate and make impressive promises. But if my faith is real, it means trusting things to go His way and according to His timing. So what about you? Are you trusting God for real or dictating what should happen? Are you putting your faith to work or trying to manipulate the process? Are you talking faith but crossing your fingers? Trust God's heart and His best intentions. No matter how He chooses to work things out, His ways are best.

Mar 24, 2017, 4:04 PM

When you are GOD'S GRATEFUL GIRL, it is not hard to find things to be grateful for and laugh about when you are in the hospital:-

1) My doctor told me "I come to this room to get HOPE"
2) I have 'church' & great conversation with my Chaplain
3) The food is not yummy but it is nutritious (plus I get treats)
4) The daily blood draw is no fun but it signals my party time

5) It gets boring but I have an awesome room with a view
6) I might have gotten lost on my walk but it felt like I was at the gym
7) I had weight loss on my 2017 plan and it is happening
8) My pillowcases are in love with my hair, good thing I like wigs
9) Grateful the bed is beside the bathroom, you should see me run
10) I have officially conquered getting my gown on without help

Mar 26, 2017, 7:24 PM

Saturday was rough!! I cried a lot (day and night). 'Alone, angry and afraid' summed up my feelings. But as Saturday turned into Sunday, a weight lifted and Father God poured in today's GRACE. I sang out loud all day, put makeup on and one of my wigs. I needed to look at this PRETTY PATIENT and remember that I am doing this like a BOSS, like a gorgeous girl going through this season of life. I needed to look at this PRETTY PATIENT and remember that I have conquered big things before and came out like a champ. I needed to look at this PRETTY PATIENT and encourage myself with dreams of a future that is so bright I can't even tell people what I believe God has in store for me. 'Alone, angry and afraid' are still valid feelings which I will not deny or dismiss, but I also feel BEAUTIFUL, BOLD, BLESSED and a woman beating cancer one step at a time.

Mar 29, 2017, 5:26 AM

AFTER ANOTHER SLEEPLESS NIGHT FILLED WITH INTERRUPTIONS AND ISSUES, I DID NOT KNOW WHAT TO SAY TO GOD OR HOW TO SAY IT IN THE RIGHT WAY, THEN A FRIEND SENT ME THIS SONG AND IT SAYS IT ALL. IT'S BEEN ONE FULL MONTH IN THE HOSPITAL AND I AM SCREAMING ON THE INSIDE

WANTING TO GO BACK TO MY HAVEN OF A HOME AND REGULAR LIFE, I AM TIRED LITERALLY, EMOTIONALLY, PHYSICALLY...GOD I CAN'T RUSH YOU BUT PLEASE HURRY UP!

NEED YOU NOW (How Many Times) by Plumb (official lyric video) (https://www.youtube.com/watch?v=9ylnx0NA9X4&fb-clid=IwAR3OwvHTUwwbHZ5Uylm-6sUuAOFz6TqsEZ6fyxxTJkoy-GyvuZZBoK8svtsY)

I want to believe there's beauty here
'Cause oh, I get so tired of holding on
I can't let go, I can't move on
I want to believe there's meaning here

How many times have you heard me cry out
"God please take this"?
How many times have you given me strength to
Just keep breathing?
Oh I need you
God, I need you now.

Standing on a road I didn't plan
Wondering how I got to where I am
I'm trying to hear that still small voice
I'm trying to hear above the noise

Mar 30, 2017, 6:47 PM

Some people have faith and pray with fingers crossed (uncertain more than hopeful about what is being prayed for). Here's how I CHOOSE to see my FAITH (especially in this season)—Which child who has a great relationship with his/her Dad/Mom doubt when they are told what they will get for Christmas or that special birthday gift? A child usually takes it for granted that WHAT DADDY/MOMMY SAID THEY WILL DO, WILL BE DONE!!! (Simple sincere childlike faith). So that is where I am in my faith right now. It may make no sense to you, I may seem naive or in denial to you, BUT I AM GOD'S CHILD, HIS GRATEFUL GIRL AND I CHOOSE TO BELIEVE THAT HS IS ABLE TO DO MORE THAN I CAN ASK OR THINK. HE KNOWS WHAT I DESIRE AND WHAT I AM HOPING FOR, SO I AM GOING TO TRUST HIM ALL THE WAY. HE IS ALL I HAVE, MY ONLY GUARANTEE, MY ONLY OPTION SO I WILL PUT ALL MY EGGS IN HIS BASKET AND TRUST HIM WITH MY CHILDLIKE FAITH!!

Apr 2, 2017, 7:53 PM

REFLECT CHRIST IN YOUR CRISIS—I am choosing to rejoice even though it is not always easy. This hospital stay has been over a month, not counting the previous ones. But God knows the when, why, what, where, who and how, so I choose to reflect Him. Keep praying, praising, trusting and believing.

Apr 3, 2017, 11:34 PM

Discharged and back at my home!!! "Mommy I missed you" were the best words I heard today. After being confined for over a month, it felt great to be in traffic, pick up DJ from school, have mommy-kids time, use my own bathroom, watch my DVR shows, eat with the family at the dining table, listen to the soft hum of the washing machine, have supper then tuck my son in to bed. These are things I will never take for granted again.

Apr 4, 2017, 9:07 PM

"Mama, mama you know I love you"—I had no idea that at this age and stage in my life, mommy would be the person here for me, providing the GIFT OF PRESENCE AND PEACE. I had no idea that once again, she would see it fit to give of herself to care for a cancer patient (because she already did that with daddy—you know, the "for better or worse, sickness and health" promise she made). I had no idea that she would be the relative friend who God would choose to be His hands and heart, prepare the meals I need, send the photos and phone updates, share the laughter and love that would assure me I am not alone in this. Yet, God knew she was equipped to walk this road with me and be His light, His love, and His reassurance that I've got someone. God knew that her time caring for daddy would prepare her to care for me. Honestly, I wish God did not give this to her again, but He knew that I needed the VERY BEST AND THE STRONGEST so He asked mommy to step up again and take on this assignment which will show forth His glory. My prayer is that God will grant her double for her trouble like He did for Job. May He see it fit to bless and honor her privately and publicly. May Father God give her continued health, maintain her beautiful youthful look, give her the desires of her heart, restore in special ways, bless her with tangible things and pour out opportunities that dazzle her. May He answer her prayers for my total healing and all her requests for her children and grandchildren. May all the time she has sacrificed be rewarded and all the service she has given be repaid in this life. May she know that my heart loves her now more than ever and that this time of care will be blessed because she is choosing to give me the GIFT OF PRESENCE AND PEACE. #GratefulDaughter #BlessedMother #ILoveHerSoMuch

Apr 13, 2017, 4:31 PM

Most of my hair is gone and I am ready to rock the various looks as I make the BEST of this cancer-chemo situation. It took me a few days to get used to this and feel ok with the new look, but I remembered that I am so much more than my hair, skin, weight, etc. My soul rejoices in THE ONE who makes me beautiful, bold and blessed (all because of His grace).

Apr 21, 2017, 6:01 AM

"SHHHHH, shut up, sugarcoat it, spiritualize it, stay silent about it, Your truth makes me uncomfortable so don't speak about it." Sadly, this is the response (vibe, feeling) that many people get when others are incapable of handling our tough truth. For me, this candid sharing about my experiences with cancer (#ConqueringCancerChronicles) does not sit well with everyone because many people have attached stigma and shame to sickness. For others, the sharing of their real raw feelings and experiences cause others to flinch (in offense) and flee (detach and disconnect) because they are unwilling to hear and uncomfortable dealing with the realities of people's pain and suffering. Church people tend to do that—over spiritualize to avoid confronting real situations or stop communicating altogether, instead of dealing with things for what they really are. Accepting things for what they really are does not negate the faith walk, neither does it ignore the truth that God is able to handle all things. Instead people (especially church people) need to grow up, get real and allow people to be honest about their (our) feelings and experiences. Being a Christian does not mean we get a pass and will never experience sickness, sadness, suffering, trials, tragedy, tribulations, etc. A CANCER DIAGNOSIS CAN CHANGE ANYONE'S LIFE IN ONE DAY (I am currently living that reality). In the same token, financial loss, divorce, incarceration, accident, death of a loved one, rape, terminal illness, etc. can blindside you and affect YOUR life in a moment. Therefore, have a heart of care and compassion when those who are dealing with difficult things need to speak and share. Be mature and wise to give place for people's honest revelations and expressions. Many of us are grappling with gigantic life changing situations and must process the tough decisions. While I agree that there is an appropriate way for this kind of self-expression and disclosure (not everything should be shared on social media or with certain people), I have chosen to share my #ConqueringCancerChronicles on Facebook as a way to inform, update, encourage and inspire all of those who genuinely care, those who are merely curious and even the ones who are cynical and critical about my journey. Any way this process goes, God is directing the path and remains in control of the outcome. As you pray for me and others, remember that people in pain (physical and emotional) need a place where free expression can take place without being silenced, stifled, shamed or shunned. Allow us to speak and share our truth with the hope that people will be informed and inspired.

Until next time,

SHANNAN

Apr 22, 2017, 4:02 PM

I have decided to make the best of what others see as a 'bad' situation—It is a matter of perspective, attitude, and childlike faith in Father God. No one thing defines me (no sickness, no flaw, no failure, no success, no degree, no title, no trait, no season, no setback). #MyChoiceToRejoice #AttitudeBegetsAltitude #ConqueringCancer

Apr 23, 2017, 7:50 PM

As I mentally prepare to be readmitted and begin the next phase of this journey, I want to let you know that I am at peace and okay, not because I don't feel scared or annoyed sometimes, but because God has been giving me GRACE for this faith walk.

Little did I know that my 2016 end of year plan to do professional video blogs was going to take this turn as I record these #ConqueringCancerChronicles. God saw that this was going to be a good way to launch me into my next season, so I am going along with His plan, process and purpose. I am not in denial about the severity of the diagnoses, the toll it can take, the things that could be affected or how long this entire journey could be. On the contrary, I am aware of the possibilities and accept God's way of accomplishing His plans and fulfilling His purposes, even if it is not our desired outcome. Therefore, I am going to remain vibrant and vivacious when I feel like it, cry my eyes out when I need to, fuss and fight with the Lord when it is necessary, and basically keep it real during each part of the journey. I am a miracle in the making and my testimony will give God glory.

#ConqueringCancer #SharingMyFaithWalk

All for God's glory,

SHANNAN

Apr 26, 2017, 7:10 AM

Praying over the chemo bags, calling the names of my friends who are also going through chemotherapy and other cancer treatments, stretching my hand and lifting my faith for all of us. Each person's cancer diagnosis and treatment plan is different and unique. Cancer is not always a death sentence or indicative of our promotion to Heaven. Sometimes, cancer is God's ways of saying, "I need to use your body and mind to show you and others what you are really made of and what I can do. I need to use this process to remind people that I AM GOD AND I AM ABLE TO DO MORE THAN YOU ALL CAN ASK OR IMAGINE. I AM

GOING TO USE YOU TO DISPLAY MY GLORY. WATCH AS I ALLOW YOUR BODY TO TOLERATE THESE TREATMENTS, MINIMIZE SIDE EFFECTS, BRING THE RIGHT SUPPORTERS, PROVIDE YOUR DAILY NEEDS, GIVE STRENGTH AND GRACE FOR THE LONG HAUL. WATCH AS I USE THIS TO GLORIFY MY NAME AND BLESS OTHERS. I'VE GOT YOU TROOPER, YOU WILL GET THROUGH THIS. I AM HERE WITH YOU!!!!

Hang in there my fellow cancer conquerors!! We will get through this by the Grace of God. However this goes, know that He has already designated the required GRACE for each part of the process. I stand with you all today (you know who you are, no tagging needed for privacy sake). Love and blessings!!

SHANNAN #ConqueringCancerChronicles

Apr 28, 2017, 5:06 AM
HOW TO HELP A PATIENT OR SOMEONE DEALING WITH THE LOSS OF A LOVED ONE (click on YouTube Link as well)

My 4 A.M. Annoyed But Helpful Post–Don't read this if you don't want to hear MY TRUTH right now or if these posts offend you:

I had one of my worst days in the hospital yesterday and I am so over this entire process (the financial cost that is required and is adding up, the uncertainty of everything, the daily demands on my body, the fatigue, the swelling from all the liquids going in at rapid rates for hours at a time, the things I can't eat, the constant restroom trips, the unsteadiness on my feet, the lack of control over what all these medications are doing, the lack of a guaranteed treatment plan, the daily blood draws, the limited access to normal life).

It got me thinking about ways people can truly help a cancer patient (seeing that I am now connected to several like myself) and those who have recently lost a loved one (because the death angel seems to be very busy lately). As I replay Sheryl Sandberg's (Facebook's COO's) interview with Ellen a few days ago, (watch the short YouTube video in the comment section) I feel the need to share some of her thoughts and add mine based on this experience and my morning annoyance:

REAL WAYS TO HELP A CANCER PATIENT OR SOMEONE DEALING WITH A SERIOUS SICKNESS:

- When you find out, SAY SOMETHING, because your silence speaks volumes and it is not often interpreted well by the sick person. If you think it is hard for you to acknowledge what is happening to them because of how much you feel sad, hurt or helpless, triple that and try to imagine what your 'friend' family member, church member, associate is really dealing with. Your silence sucks right now and it could severely damage whatever relationship you used to have when your words, concern and care are needed right now (not later, now—find something to say)

- If you don't know what to say and you are a Christian who prays, OFFER TO PRAY REGULARLY and actually let them know you are praying (not just a one time obligatory "I am praying for you" so you can cross that off your list), but really pray and let them know you are standing with them in prayer

- Don't ask "Let me know what I can do for you" because that places the pressure on the patient to go figure out what is feasible for you to do. Be practical and prayerful BUT DO SOMETHING (A friend of mine ordered makeup and mailed to my home so that I will always feel like a girly girl whenever I want to. I appreciate that gift so much because it helps me mentally. Someone paid a bill so that I would not have to worry myself about that one, another person brought me beet juice, others brought me Jamaican breakfast when I needed high iron foods, my students packed goodie boxes for my kids, and so many have stepped up with practical things that help). Pray about what you can do for your cancer/sick friends so they don't have to figure out what is best for you to do (that is too hard for us right now)

- DON'T PREPARE US FOR DEATH because we live with that possibility every day. Making light of our mortality or subtly shoving it in our minds is not helpful while we are fighting to live for as long as we can. We know where this could lead so we want to live as long as we can, not in denial but making the best of all the days we have. Don't bring it up if it is not time for that conversation or if you are not close to us emotionally and spiritually to have that candid talk

- In the same token, DON'T MAKE LIGHT OF OUR DIAGNOSIS as though you are aware of what is taking place in our bodies. Every cancer and serious sickness is different and requires a unique plan, so don't be eager to suggest things that may not work with what our doctors are doing. Not every solution is right for us and we need to be able to refuse care or receive care based on what we feel is best for our situation

- PLEASE TREAT US LIKE WE ARE MORE THAN JUST A PATIENT who can still function well in most settings. I don't know what I would do if I could not log in from time to time and stay connected with my job, make decisions at home and still feel useful. Just because I am a cancer patient it does not mean I can no longer make a valuable contribution to my home, work, church and community.

- PLEASE UNDERSTAND THAT WE ARE MORE WORRIED AND CONCERNED ABOUT OUR CHILDREN AND CAREGIVERS than you could ever realize. I am more concerned about how all this is affecting my children and family than I am about the diagnoses and my treatment. It is important to me that they are as ok as can be because they see and experience a lot of this firsthand and there is not much I can do to help them. That is hard in this situation, so if you can help with children and caregivers that helps the patient

- DON'T LEAVE US OUT AS IF WE ARE NO LONGER NECESSARY OR INTERESTED IN WHAT IS GOING ON. If you used to include us in church announcements, work emails, family updates, jokes, games, etc., keep on doing so because we need to feel relevant and needed, we need to stay informed and in the know, we need to feel like we still matter in your world

REAL WAYS TO HELP WHEN A LOVED ONE HAS PASSED ON

- DON'T PREACH OR OVER-SPIRITUALIZE TO THE ONES WHO ARE DEALING WITH THE DEATH as if they don't know that their loved one is now resting in Heaven (it sounds good but is not what is needed in that moment)

- GIVE THEM PERMISSION TO FEEL, CRY, EXPRESS, TALK AND DEAL WITH THE LOSS THE BEST WAYS THEY NEED TO. Don't tell them not to cry or scold them if they need to grieve in ways that you don't understand. Allow the remaining loved ones to get through the initial mourning the best ways they see fit

- RESPECT THEIR NEED FOR PRIVACY AND THEIR DECISION ABOUT HOW TO HONOR THEIR LOVED ONE. This is not about you but about what they need to do in their hearts

- OFFER THE GIFT OF YOUR PRESENCE AND PRESENTS depending on the nature of your relationship. Be practical and sensitive about what is needed to support them at this time

- SHARE THE HAPPY MEMORIES YOU HAD WITH THEIR LOVED ONE and validate their impact in your life

- STICK AROUND AND CHECK IN REGULARLY AFTER THE INITIAL GRIEVING PERIOD HAS ENDED. They feel the loss greatly after the service and people no longer come around

May 1, 2017 at 8:20 PM

Thanks for YOUR PRAYERS and POSITIVE WORDS. To those of you who really prayed me through and connected with me today, THANK YOU!! Jesus Almighty—this gets heavy sometimes!!! The emotional and spiritual toll this takes is no joke. A body that feels and looks different is scary. A future that is uncertain frightens the hell out of me. But I was just reminded that NOTHING WILL ACCESS OR AFFECT ME WITHOUT GOD'S PERMISSION AND IT IS OK TO BE WEAK AND GIVE IN TO THE HANDICAP SO THAT GOD'S STRENGTH CAN BE SEEN. Somehow, it is all working for my good and God's glory, so I sigh again, smile again, accept this again and try again to go through every part of this process (even though it is frightening and frustrating). #ConqueringCancerChronicles

May 3, 2017, 11:58 PM

Dedicated to my fellow patients and mothers who are con-quering life one fight at a time.—Please take your time with her.

She is wired that way because she has to develop grit and gut for the biggest fight of her life. Allow her to become what she needs to be. You could not handle what she will have to carry and conquer. And you will never comprehend her training process. Give her space and respect. She is on assignment for the kingdom of Heaven.

Jun 6, 2017, 9:42 AM

That moment your Nurse Tech comes in to introduce herself and says, "Oh my God you're so young. What are you, like 28? Girl you are going to run right through this. God is good."

Then yesterday my Chaplain comes in and after sharing said, "I came in here to comfort you, but you are the one comforting me. Can you pray for me please?"

I AM ON ASSIGNMENT—MAKING GOD PROUD

Jun 7, 2017, 4:30 PM

Can you pray the 'NEVERTHELESS' prayers? Can you see the good in the midst of the bad? Can you choose to be thankful instead of taking things and people for granted? Time for self-reflection—times are too serious not to do so. #ConqueringCancer

Jun 10, 2017, 11:45 AM

Another chemo-hospital week completed and God is smiling through these faces. Closer to conquering cancer, closer to complete healing, closer to all God's promises. SMILE PEOPLE, you are more blessed than you realize. LIVE LIFE LOUD, MAKE GOD PROUD!!

Jun 20, 2017, 4:26 PM

I've been quiet, questioning, quarreling...104 fever is dangerous so I've been back in the hospital since Saturday, fighting.

Weak, weary, worried, wondering. It's been 6 months and I have seen a total change of life. So much more on the verge of happening unless God gives me a 'late in the midnight hour turnaround miracle'. I respect His desire and trust His plan, but Lord... this (all of it, not just my condition) is heavy to bear. The emotional toll this is taking on me, mommy and Allie is rough. Why did the Bible say women are the weaker vessel? We are having to be strong, so strong, even when we are on empty. And if the next treatment in this plan occurs, it is going to get harder for us. Would you pray that God gives us a break to breathe, a reprieve, a relief from all that is happening? Would you pray that God begins to answer with clarity and specificity? Would you pray that God will be more real to the three of us like He was with the 3 Hebrews boys? Would you pray that kind caring friends and ministry leaders would see the need to connect with my mommy now just like she and dad did for others? Would you pray that every need will be met especially going into this next phase? Would you wrap us in your heart?

Weary Warrior

Shannan

Jun 29, 2017, 1:31 AM

Many never understood me (the sometimes messy yet magnificent me who sought the Lord). Now in this season, I understand why I always had this drive and desperation for the Lord. I understand why a pair of spike heel shoes limited my ability to dance in praise. I never knew that I would have these restrictions that would prevent me from giving God my kind of praise—rapid heart rate, needing a mask and soon I won't be able to go to church. I am limited to a room and my inner praise as I sing songs like "We lift our hands Lord here in your presence we worship you" and "Be God here as you are in Heaven" and "There's a remnant in the room and we're crying out for you". My friends, seek God while He may be found. Adjust your priorities and work schedules to accommodate quality time for prayer, praise and the Word. Get involved in your local church and make sure your children take their rightful places too (not on devices but paying attention so they can grow in the things of God). You don't know when your day of a diagnosis or disability is coming, so make use of your freedoms now. Stop taking church and the things of God for granted. Stop bragging in 'church flow' pics if we are not going to see what other good things are flowing from your church attendance and walk with the Lord. Stop acting like you can't move in church when you shake your tail feather for your jam or sports team. This time, do it differently and seek all of God, give Him your best and don't wait until it is too late.

Hospital bed appeal

From an eager worshipper–SHANNAN.

Jul 3, 2017, 10:41 AM

What's on my mind? Let's see...

I am still grateful for all the little BIG things. I no longer have research papers to grade, admissions interviews with applicants or staff meetings, but my mind is still alert and I am preparing for GOD'S NEXT BEST. I can't be with people for my safety but I get to share special moments with the key ones. I don't have a lot of regrets because even the messy moments helped to make me who I am (nothing wasted). I still have great expectations for GOD'S NEXT BEST even though I don't know exactly when it will begin and what it will be like. I don't have hate in my heart (disappointment about things and some people, but not hate) because hate is a heavy burden to bear and Lord knows, I don't have time or emotional energy to waste. I have no choice but to trust and rely on the Lord and the people He has entrusted to care for me. When it's all said and done, I love my Lord. I am HIS daughter, He's in charge (even when I wonder if His hands are still directing my life). Yes, I am still grateful for all the little BIG things because those are the ones that really matter.

Jul 10, 2017, 8:36 PM

I chose not to do a birthday countdown (reflective inspiring posts) this year because I am numb. IF ANYONE TOLD ME LAST YEAR THAT THIS YEAR WOULD BRING ALL OF THIS BEFORE MY BIRTHDAY (cancer, no income, government applications for aid, deemed disabled, weak most of the time, watching others live their lives, unable to participate in most activities or attend events, trying to be strong for everybody while I face the realities of my current situation), I PROBABLY WOULD HAVE RESPONDED LIKE MADEA!!!! Yet here I am, 2 days before my BIG day and I am numb, alone, afraid, walking through this strange new routine like the lead character in a movie I never knew I was being cast for. BUT IN SPITE OF ALL THIS, I WILL PRAISE HIM IN MY HEART. I have nothing profound to post as a countdown (thanks to my Facebook Memories, I realized that I posted quite a bit of solid stuff through the years). I am not this super person some of you seem to see (I'm simply trying to take my reality and have the best attitude about it). IN MY NUMBNESS I WILL FIND SOME COMFORT IN SONGS OF PRAISE THAT I STILL HAVE LIFE, HOPE, MOMMY, ALLIE, OTTY, SHANEL, DJ and the family friends who have been here for me (in real meaningful ways). This year, I don't even want a cake—I want results, I want to feel different, I want strength, I want good medical reports, I want to get better, I want good life,

I want to know my bills will be taken care of, I want people who really care about me, I want God's healing virtue to show up, I want to be made whole, I want to praise and dance like I used to...no cake, just a few wishes/wants. In the meantime, I go to a quiet place of praise and worship.

#GODHAVEMERCY #PRAISEISWHATIDO

Jul 31, 2017, 3:49 PM

THANKS AND TANTRUM—When I recorded this earlier today, I was in great spirits but now I am in my bed crying hysterically with the weight of all that is about to happen. Transplant team just called and this could happen sooner than I imagined. "God, are you sure this is the way we should go in light of all that comes with the pre and post transplant process? How am I going to pay my monthly COBRA to ensure I retain insurance? How am I going to pay my rent and bills? How do you expect me to go through this process as if I am not already exhausted? How do you expect me to keep showing strength as if I am not human? You are the only close male presence/figure in my life so I don't have anyone else to thank or throw a tantrum. (Feeling like Job and Elijah right now—this assignment is heavy—Journey part-ners, I could use prayers right now please!!!!!!) #TiredOfThis #IsItTooLateForAMiracle #IHateThis #LordHelpMePlease #ForgiveMyWeakness #LonelyJourney

Aug 6, 2017, 9:38 AM

There are 2 things that are dangerous for a cancer patient—stress and fever (I had both last night). So you can imagine my joy when twice last night I woke up to see my son standing over me praying. My kids are troopers who are dealing with a lot but they make me proud to see their commitment to the things of God.

Recently while having her devotion, Shanel came to my room to get a communion cup to include in her time of worship. Please pray for them that God will guard their hearts, honor their efforts and cover them in all things. Nelly Blair and DJ are my medicine, my motivation and my reason for striving to be a true Christian in my attitudes and actions.

Aug 14, 2017, 5:13 PM

Necessary Transportation—I never knew how much I would appreciate the use of a wheelchair but I realize that in this season, there are times when it is a necessary means of transportation. You may not need to use a wheelchair but perhaps your current circumstances will be the necessary transportation to transition you from one stage of life to another. Your storm may be the mode of transportation to shift you to the next season. Don't be too quick to resent your situation because it could be your necessary means of transportation.

Aug 17, 2017, 10:58 PM

Testimony & Prayer Request (https://www.youtube.com/watch?v=L__CeDpJsew)

"Shannan, there is no more leukemia found in your system"—GLORY HALLELUJAH!!! Thank you for praying and believing. Please praise God with me, then pray for the next phase of the journey (whether it be an 11th hour supernatural miracle or the scheduled transplant). Get your glory God, do your thing Father, your daughter submits to your plan, your daughter is preparing for greater purpose. "If you can use anything Lord, you can use me" #ConqueringCancer #IAmOnAssignment #VictoryBelongsToJesus

Aug 18, 2017, 3:34 PM

I am honored to have a team of ladies who have stepped up to join mommy as caregivers and drivers. Zaneen Thompson and Ms. Cathy Farmer-Kindell attended the mandatory Caregivers Training Class. (Thank you my sister friends!!!!) We will teach the others at a later time but for now, we all feel informed and empowered about the transplant and the recovery process. God handpicked these and other ladies who met the qualification:- prayer warriors, caring hearts that show the love of Christ, faith talkers/ walkers, emotionally sensitive and safe, feel called to this assignment, love my family and are willing to show it in practical ways, they see this as ministry and service to the Lord, and they have proven that they know how to love me well. #GratefulForPresence #GladGodPickedTheRightOnes

Aug 20, 2017, 2:37 PM

Significant Sunday—Today was my last time attending a church service for a few months until I am cleared by my doctors that I can return to church. However, if a supernatural miracle stops the scheduled transplant then none of this will even matter. Nevertheless, not my will but God's will be done in all of this. It felt great to stand in church and give God passionate praise with people all around. Incidentally, this is also the last time that I will be receiving visitors for a while because after this point, I will have to limit contact with most people. Thanks to everyone who came to see me during these 8 months. Now I submit to the season of semi-isolation and trust the process that God has laid out for me and my medical team. (By the way, be careful what you pray for—you see all the weight I have lost? I started 2017 determined to lose 20lbs—I did, but not the way I wanted. LOL, still grateful though) #OnToTheNextPhase #PurposefulProcess #AllForHisGlory

Aug 22, 2017, 6:38 AM

Please bring my babies to JESUS!!! This photo collage was done last August and now one year later, my grown up babies are having to be tough troopers. The mistake we often make is to ignore how intuitive and intelligent kids are. We underestimate their ability to sense, see and process internally. Years ago, I walked the parking lot at my job crying and praying that God would raise up people who would be willing to love on and care for Shanel and Daniel. So intercessors and people who love me for real, please pray for my babies. I AM MORE CONCERNED ABOUT MY CHILDREN THAN I AM ABOUT CANCER!!! This Momma Bear is hurting deeply for my babies as they deal with their fears and frustrations, so I need help as I prepare to make room in my mind for the biggest battle of my life (going through and recovering from a risky transplant). I am confident that Shanel and Daniel will emerge with tenacity and testimonies, but in the meantime, they need spiritual and emotional reinforcements from people who know how to pray, love and care properly. Thank you in advance!!!

Aug 22, 2017, 8:59 PM

'What's on your mind?' is the prompt that Facebook uses to encourage us to share a status. Here's mine as I prepare for surgery in the morning, days of radiation and chemotherapy, followed by a transplant:

~ I never knew so many people loved and cared for me: God needed me to know that

~ I now know that several never truly loved or cared for me; it was conditional based on what they wanted me to be or do; not because I was ME (sweet salty messy magnificent flawed fabulous inspiring insecure broken beautiful hurting helpful)

~ I am glad that I went through tough times because I have a heart of compassion, can show empathy & encourage others

~ I was never disqualified from the cleansing and healing Blood of Jesus; it makes me appreciate that He thought I was worth it

~ I learned how to be resilient and optimistic at the feet of Jesus (many times I just climbed onto His lap and let Him love on me)

~ I went through many spiritual surgeries to get to where I am now so I don't take my journey, growth or God's mercy for granted

~ I have so much more growing to do but when you see me now, I am not the person I used to be or who you used to know

~ I am grateful for the times I experienced little, lack and loss because it taught me how to be content and resourceful

~ I have real friends that are more like family and that is a wonderful realization

~ I don't know what the next few days/weeks/ months will be like but I expect God to surprise me and keep me smiling

~ I have to keep asking God to guard my heart so I don't tell some people what I really think about them; my disappointment bucket has overflowed not because I expect people to be perfect beings but because there was an expectation of concern, care and consideration (this is cancer not the common cold)

~ I release the possibility that things could have gone in a different way and trust God with the past, present and future

~ I am better because of this season and for that I am grateful; where others see a death sentence, I see God's hands doing amazing things through me and to me. I am more alive and on fire now that I have been in a long time

~ I have strangers who have demonstrated more of JESUS to me than many who claim to know Jesus (I now doubt people's sincerity about their love for the Lord—weak testimonies)

~ I never believe when some people say they were too busy to see or speak to me (they just chose other priorities and shifted loyalties thinking I would not realize that was their way of avoiding me)

~ I am not the BEST person in the world but I am committed to being the BEST SHANNAN in my spheres of influence

~ I forgive easier than I used to because God forgives me all the time, plus unforgiveness is poison to oneself. But I use wisdom:- Forgiveness granted, access denied in most cases

~ I intend to get past this stage and live the abundant amazing life AFTER THIS. I have waited too long to live that kind of life. I expect God's double double. I anticipate living a life that honors the Lord. I trust in Him completely (even when it is hard to do so).

THAT WAS ROUGH... BUT GOD WILL CARRY ME THROUGH THIS PART TOO!!!!

Aug 23, 2017, 8:42 PM

Day 1–THAT WAS ROUGH. So it appears that radiation does not like me and I don't like it either. BUT GOD WILL CARRY ME THROUGH THIS PART TOO!!!! I am not going to interact as much with my phone for the next few days, so please understand and keep praising for victory (ability to tolerate all of this, fever to go away, and minimal side effects). Thanks for caring!!!

Aug 24, 2017, 1:50 PM

I didn't wake up from surgery singing this time, but Alecia Ellis' post gave me a sweet reminder of why I am inclined to worship through it all. Our dad was not just a worshipper in the pulpit. He modeled it at home and in the car too. So as children we saw a pastor who praised not only when he was on a platform. He was so ahead of his time, that he introduced us to contemporary 'Praise and Worship' songs (before it became popular). We learned how to worship while doing chores as a family on Saturday mornings (he was also doing chores with us). We learned how to praise and pray in family devotions. I learned God could answer prayers when he held my vomit bucket as cramps tore through my body as he prayed. It's no wonder 'Praise is what I do' even in this season because my daddy (and mommy) taught us in the home. I just came out of surgery and am praising now because it's what I know will work in every situation. If your children only see you worship at church, then you are missing many moments to teach them that praise and worship should not be confined to your church building. They need to learn how to pray and praise in the midst of trouble and triumph. #Groggybutgrateful #Sorebutsinging #Painbutpraising

Aug 25, 2017, 11:09 AM
Common sense reminders from my hospital bed –

1. Get out of the way, let go of pride and allow the experts to help you (I am not used to getting help to go to the bathroom or bathe). Some of us will never get better or receive inner healing because we refuse to be helped by counselors, pastors, mentors, and people with experience who see that we need help.
2. Stop fighting the sleep and let the meds work. Being sleepy all the time is new to me as I find myself fighting the sleep like babies do. (Some of us act as though if we allow our bodies and minds to rest, we are going to miss out on life's greatest moments). When your body needs the rest, close your eyes and rest.
3. Turn off or silence the noise from devices (when you are a patient, you should not respond immediately to every notification on your phone). In the same token, don't be too quick to reply, react or respond to every news or provocation that comes your way. Not everything or everyone needs to be acknowledged.

Sometimes they are the things being sent by the enemy to distract and disturb your peace of mind. Shut off the noise makers.

Aug 28, 2017, 1:22 AM
OUR TESTIMONY –

Written to my sister because of all the things we have gone through and the things we are about to go through:-WE HAVE A GOD WHO SEES, KNOWS AND CARES!!

For everything that happened that could have tugged us from His keeping care, God said "BACK UP, SHE BELONGS TO ME AND HER SOUL IS KEPT."

For everyone who turned and walked away, God said "GO BOUT YU BUSINESS, YOU ARE NOT NEEDED HERE BECAUSE YOU NO LONGER KNOW HOW TO KEEP WHAT I ENTRUSTED TO YOU."

For every struggle that came to shake us from a place of certainty, God said, "GO AWAY FOR I KNOW HOW TO KEEP WHAT IS COMMITTED TO ME IN A PLACE OF STABILITY AND CERTAINTY."

HE IS THE KEEPER OF OUR SOULS AND ALL THAT PERTAINS TO US!!! GOD WILL MAKE A WAY AND GET US THROUGH ALL OF THIS.

#BedtimeThoughts #KeptByJesus

Aug 29, 2017, 5:39 PM

The reason some folks can't support you publicly is because of the things they thought and said about you privately. I observed as people made their comments about the situation in Texas with the mega-church pastor, and was reminded of how eager we are to run with bits and pieces of information as we bash people's character. We quickly forget all the good a person does and latch on to fragmented information (some false, some true but not the full story). The lesson I got from this latest uproar is that some people will not say anything good about you because of how much bad they said about you. Don't allow their willingness and eagerness to jump on the bandwagon of gossip, cynical comments and rude remarks to disturb your peace or change the good person that you are. Keep on living, giving, sharing, caring, hoping and praying. God knows how to handle those who sow discord, dish out dishonor and dare to speak against His work in you. Do good, be good!!!

#PeopleNeedTheLord   #DontSeekTheirSupport #LetYourActionSpeak

Aug 30, 2017, 3:35 PM

Part II of the process is done. Alecia Ellis' surgery went well. Mommy

LadyJoyce has both daughters admitted in the hospital but Dawn Martin is here to support us. I felt honored to leave my room to come hang out in her room. But more than anything, I am grateful that God saw this coming and gave me the right mommy, donor sister, brother, children and support system equipped to go through this. Hallelujah!! Glory to God!!

Aug 31, 2017, 4:34 AM

It is 4 a.m. on the morning of my bone marrow transplant (or as the medical team calls it, my new birthday). I could record a video but my HEROINE MOTHER is sleeping on her sofa bed. It is also daddy's birthday!!! Only God could have scheduled this to occur on August 31st—He is such an intentional planner!! Lol!!! I am calm, reflective, grateful and hopeful.

Mommy's prayer is that when the cells get together, they will meet, greet, recognize their purpose and come together without competing or fighting. As I thought about her prayer, it dawned on me that the reason many relationships don't work (spouses, pastor and worship leader, employer and effective employees, etc.) is that they fail to recognize their true roles. Instead of coming together to help fulfill destiny and purpose, extend the life of the relationship and prevent catastrophe, they get territorial, put up resistance, become competitive, act out in negative ways, exhibit signs of resentment and prevent the manifestation of real purpose and progress.

It is my prayer, like LadyJoyce Wallace, that when the transplant is done today, the "critical 100 days after" will result in good reports. I pray that my body will not reject and fight against the very cells meant to bring healing and wholeness. I pray that my recovery will not take as long as is normally projected but will go according to God's timetable. I pray that the Blood of Jesus will give me a divine supernatural blood transfusion so that this never happens again and I will have a long healthy happy life!! #IAmReady #AbundantLife #AllForGodsGlory

Aug 31, 2017, 9:53 AM

Greeting my darling donor Alecia Ellis before the cell harvesting process. Grateful to God, everyone (and everything) He is using to make this happen. All for His glory!!! Happy New Birthday to me!!!

Aug 31, 2017, 8:56 PM

IT IS FINISHED AND IT WENT WELL!!
WE ARE RESTING NOW—PRAISE THE LORD!!!

Chapter 20

Bone Marrow Transplant

The cancer journey officially ended in August of 2017, but being in remission heralded the beginning of another significant part of the healing and recovery process. Without a bone marrow transplant, perhaps I would not be alive today sharing my story with you. According to Be The Match website, "There are over 70 diseases that can be treated with a bone marrow transplant" (bethematch.org, 2017), so one of my new life goals is to do my part to inform and increase awareness to as many people as I can. People often fear what they don't know or wait until it is too late to get information. I now have a responsibility as a bone marrow transplant recipient to share for those who will need a second chance at life and for the many who need to register to become potential donors. I hope you will never need a transplant but if you do or know someone who does, my prayer is that my experience will be informative and inspirational.

Several months before the bone marrow transplant, both of my siblings were tested to see if they were a match. It required them traveling to Moffitt Cancer Center to get their cheeks swabbed. My medical insurance covered the cost, so they did not have a financial obligation for this simple process. In fact, the cost of donation, if one is deemed a match, is covered by the recipient's insurance. Once my sister, Alecia's, results came back indicating that she was a match, her body was prepared weeks before the day of transplant. This included receiving shots to boost the production of cells in her body so that on the day of the transplant, her body would be ready for the harvesting process. A mandatory class was provided for caregivers and the transplant recipients prior to the actual transplant.

A bone marrow transplant sounds frightening to the person who is uninformed about what it consists of and is designed to accomplish. Simply put, the process of:

> Transplantation of blood making stem cells is used to treat certain patients with leukemia, aplastic anemia, lymphomas, solid tumors or other hematologic disorders. The source of the stem cell can be either from the bone marrow or the peripheral blood...Bone marrow is the spongy substance found inside the bones. It resembles blood and actually is the factory where stem cells develop" (Transplant Handbook, 2019).

The MedlinePlus medical encyclopedia website (2019) indicates that there are three (3) types of bone marrow transplants:

1. ***Umbilical cord blood*** – *"Stem cells are removed from a newborn baby's umbilical cord right after birth. The stem cells are frozen and stored until they are needed for a transplant."*
2. ***Autologous*** – *"The term auto means self. Stem cells are removed from you before you receive high-dose*

chemotherapy or radiation treatment. The stem cells are stored in a freezer."

3. **Allogeneic** – *"The term allo means other. Stem cells are removed from another person, called a donor. Most times, the donor's genes must at least partly match your genes. Special tests are done to see if a donor is a good match for you. A brother or sister is most likely to be a good match. Sometimes parents, children, and other relatives are good matches. Donors who are not related to you, yet still match, may be found through national bone marrow registries."*

The transplant team did an excellent job of providing the necessary information in a mandatory class for patients and their caregivers. The medical team gave us adequate information about expectations and ensured that the necessary pre-transplant treatment was done. My preparation included meeting all the criteria for an Allogeneic Bone Marrow Transplant. These included the following:

- *Valid insurance covering the entire transplant process including all medications pre- and post-transplant*
- *100% compliance in all areas including but not limited to: social, medical and behavioral*
- *A caregiver (age 18 or older) committed, willing and able to provide 24-hour care for at least 100 days post-transplant*
- *Reliable transportation for up to 365 days (no public transportation allowed due to high risk for infection)*
- *Childcare in place for up to 365 days post-transplant for patient's children aged 17 or younger*

- *Housing/lodging during transplant must be no further than 60 minutes from the transplant center for emergency purposes for at least 100 days post-transplant*
- *Clearance through extensive screening which includes, but is not limited to history and physical exam, dental clearance, pre-transplant evaluations, psychosocial assessment*

A week before the transplant day, I left home knowing that this would be a very long hospital stay because it was required that I remain under constant medical supervision for a month after transplant. I was admitted to the hospital to begin radiation treatment for three days followed by chemotherapy for four days. During that time, I underwent surgery to insert the trifusion line which would be used during my transplant.

On August 30th, I was given a day of rest and my donor-sister, Alecia, was admitted to the hospital. She also had to do surgery to insert a trifusion line through which her cells would be harvested.

Transplant Day Facebook Posts:-

Shan GratefulGirl

Aug 31, 2017, 4:34 AM

It is 4 a.m. on the morning of my bone marrow transplant (or as the medical team calls it, my new birthday). I could record a video but my HEROINE MOTHER is sleeping on her sofa bed. It is also daddy's birthday!!! Only God could have scheduled this to occur on August 31st–He is such an intentional planner!! Lol!!! I am calm, reflective, grateful and hopeful.

Mommy's prayer is that when the cells get together, they will meet, greet, recognize their purpose and come together without competing or fighting. As I thought about her prayer, it dawned on me that the reason many relationships don't work (spouses, pastor and worship leader, employer and effective employees, etc.) is that they fail to recognize their true roles. Instead of coming together to help fulfill destiny and purpose, extend the life of the relationship and prevent catastrophe, they get territorial, put up resistance, become competitive, act out in negative ways, exhibit signs of resentment and prevent the manifestation of real purpose and progress.

It is my prayer, like LadyJoyce Wallace, that when the transplant is done today, the "critical 100 days after" will result in good reports. I pray that my body will not reject and fight against the very cells meant to bring healing and wholeness. I pray that my recovery will not take as long as is normally projected but will go according to God's timetable. I pray that the Blood of Jesus will give me a divine supernatural blood transfusion so that this never happens again and I will have a long healthy happy life!! #IAmReady #AbundantLife #AllForGodsGlory

On the morning of the transplant, I went to my sister's room seeing that we were on the same floor in the hospital. Mom and our sister-friend, Dawn (who had traveled from Jamaica to care for Alecia), were attending to her. We greeted each other, sang worship songs and thanked the medical team preparing for the first phase of the transplant process – harvesting of Alecia's cells. August 31st would have been our father's 69th Earth birthday, so that fact was not lost on us that his day would become my new transplant birthday. Needless to say, this awareness made the entire process even more meaningful.

It took many hours for Alecia's cells to be harvested before I could receive them. My body needed about five (5) million cells to accomplish the transplant but we later found out that my sister's body had produced sixteen (16) million cells! I must include her Facebook post about this amazing feat a few days after she was released from the hospital.

"Mash Down That Lie"

Penned by Alecia Lewis

There was a popular political slogan in Jamaica: "Mash down that lie." It was used to refute the lies, deceptive words, agendas and contradictory schemes. This morning I heard those words ringing in my ear, "mash down that lie."

I've been careful to sleep on my left side in order to avoid rolling onto the side where the incision was made. Deep in sleep and oblivious to the wound, I rolled over to the right side and immediately felt the pain of the still aching wound. I gently placed my hand on the gauze protecting the incision and rubbed the area to soothe the pain. It was in that moment I recalled what was said to me after the Bone Marrow cell harvesting: "your body produced three times the amount of cells we needed. We only needed five million cells but you gave us sixteen million cells. Your sister now has cells that can be stored for her if she ever needs cells again."

Wait! My body did what? My body? Me? The one who has been criticized for not being able to produce?

I thought it was said I'm not good enough (mash down that lie)

I thought I heard that nothing I did amounted to anything of worth (mash down that lie)

I thought it was said I'm not a finisher (mash down that lie)

I thought that since so much time has elapsed it made no sense waiting on God to fulfill His promises (mash down that lie)

I thought I just hold others back (mash down that lie)

I thought I wasn't able to give life (mash down that lie)

I thought my illnesses would disqualify me from helping my sister (mash down that lie)

I thought God was done with me (mash down that lie)

I could list all the LIES that have been spoken to me and against me and against my destiny, but who has time for that?! God has a peculiar way of working His will and showing us just who we are and whose we are. The next time you are challenged about your identity (in Christ) simply mash down that lie. The next time someone walks away from you determining that time with you is not worth it, because you're heading nowhere simply because God has not yet allowed some things to come to fruition, let them go, don't accept the lie, mash down that lie. Above all, don't lie to yourself. Others will lie to you. Others will write you off. Others will forsake you for a better, grander, lavish life where things happen quickly and there's no need to wait. That's alright as long as you never quit on yourself. God will show up in HIS time and when He, who is Truth appears, He will MASH DOWN THAT LIE.

As my sister lay in her room delivering the cells that would become my own, I was being prepared for what was about to become my new birth. Nurses gave me medication to help alleviate the expected feelings of nausea and help me sleep before the transplant. My brother, Otty, was not able to be in the room with mom, Dawn and I, but he was thoughtful enough to grant me a wish. I wanted two things in the room when the transplant was being done – my Mother's Day photo collage cushion from my children and the sounds of my brother playing music. Otty obliged me and sought the help of several professional singers and musicians to prepare a Transplant Day Album. He even included prayers and words of comfort from a few pastors who were special to me. The sounds of jazz and reggae worship songs filled the room as I mentally prepared for what was about to take place. As my body succumbed to the medication, I took strength in the awareness that if this went well, I would be a new "baby" with a second chance at life when it was over.

A few minutes before 6 p.m., the harvested cells were brought to my room like a precious gift on Christmas morning. I was weak and sedated but managed to open my eyes and smile with gratitude that I could hold the life-giving cells in my hand.

Once the actual transplant was finished, I slipped off into a deep sleep being heavily sedated. My subconscious and spiritual self was cognizant that I would never be the same as this was indeed a new birth. I had no idea what my life and body would be like after transplant, but I slept with the assurance that God knew.

Later that night, after I woke up, my darling donor-sister visited my room to see how I was doing. As we sat side by side, we were both aware that we now have the same DNA. She marveled that her harvesting process took many hours that day, but my actual transplant was completed in less than an hour. In my frail state, I began to minister as the Holy Spirit divinely downloaded a life lesson in my system and I shared it with mom, Dawn and Alecia. This is what it looks like when process and purpose collide with destiny. It took several hours to gain the cells needed to be placed in my body, but once that was achieved, many more hours were not required for the delivery to be made. In the same way, our lives are designed to go through many processes that often take a long time. However, when the purpose for those experiences is revealed and understood, destiny is manifested and executed.

Almost a month after the transplant, my body was proving that it still knew how to fight and recalibrate as my counts were recovering faster than doctors expected. I was discharged earlier than originally anticipated.

Post-Transplant Facebook Posts:-

Sep 5, 2017, 4:05 PM
Ladies and gentlemen, I had my last chemotherapy today!!!! Now we wait for God and the body to do what must be done, then I can go home to begin recovery as an outpatient. (PRAISE BREAK)

So how should you pray? I'm glad you asked. Please pray that my counts increase quickly, I regain the ability to eat and enjoy foods, I will not have fevers, my body will regain strength quickly and that my body will not reject the new cells. Technically, I am a baby again with my sister's DNA and will need all my baby immunization shots. Pray that God will continue to provide grace, patience and provisions. Pray that no one and nothing will rob me of joy and peace. Pray that my heart will remain hidden in Christ Jesus.

Oct 7, 2017, 11:25 AM
Another 'Keep it real' post

I came to the hospital on Wednesday to do a required post-transplant procedure, expecting to go home right after. The procedure went well but I had a fever afterwards, which meant automatic admission. Yesterday I asked the Lord, "Why this unplanned admission?" Well, I got my answer in the evening. It turns out that Medicare dropped my prescription coverage without informing me. I cannot leave here until this is resolved or else I would be totally responsible for the expensive medications that I take daily. I realize that being on this side (as a patient and Medicare recipient), I am seeing with new eyes the way the system works. I am feeling compassion for my fellow Americans who are dealing with the way healthcare is provided. I am hurting for those who have no one to advocate for them as they fight tough battles. So, I will stay here until this can be resolved (through a supernatural miracle or an expedited process that reinstate my coverage). God's got this, God's got me!!!

Oct 16, 2017, 2:09 PM

Let's be honest—When most people hear that a high-priced miracle is needed, their faith shrivels and gets shy. So, this post is my request to those with AUDACIOUS FAITH. In order to be discharged with my new necessary medication, I need God to miraculously provide the $10,000 it cost or a supernatural resolution that case managers are working on. The healthcare system makes it difficult to continue prescription coverage once a disability check is sent to a patient, because that is considered income. But how can that be deemed income when a patient is unable to earn and fighting for their life? How is it we have a system that will drop the most needy preventing access to prescription coverage? Anyway, please take this urgent request to the Lord because I need my meds and $10,000 is nothing for

Him to provide. #Missingmyhome #Needhomecookedmeals #Readyforamiracle

Oct 17, 2017, 5:15 PM

Hello Shannan, how are you? Interested and caring people usually start their message that way. Here's my honest response: I am grateful to be leukemia free and progressing well post-transplant. I am weak and have difficulty walking because I lost a lot of weight. But my spirit is low now because the process has been long and I feel stuck in this healthcare prescription debacle. I pay almost $600 each month to continue coverage through COBRA only to find out that I was dropped from the system. I feel betrayed, angry, tired, bored, confused, sad and alone. Did I make God mad? Are my enemies enjoying my demise? Did I go through this journey for things to fall apart at the finish line? Does anyone understand how heavy this is and has been? Do people realize how quickly normal can change in one's life? I feel so broken. I don't take your calls after dark because I hide under my covers and don't give a rat's behind about social media. I force myself to sleep early because I am tired of the hospital routine. I silence my phone because the late night notifications jolt me out of good dreams. I soothe my mind with songs, hymns and dreams. How am I doing? I am weary and desperate for good news, relief, a new normal, tasty meals, fresh air, rain, the life you take for granted. I know it could be worse and I have not given up hope, but it's been a long season and I am broken now.

Oct 26, 2017, 6:53 AM

God provided a grant that enabled me to get the medication. On this THANKFUL THURSDAY I am grateful. Although I am still doing battle to get my prescription coverage, I pause to testify and glorify God.

Nov 24, 2017, 3:36 AM

THANKSGIVING DAY 2017—It is taking so much to share my first post-transplant pictures because it means revealing what I really look like at this point of the recovery journey. Giving THANKS and BEING REAL in this process means putting aside pride and my girly girl vanity as I respect my current restrictions and embrace the changes of my new baby body. I am not allowed to wear makeup yet, my skin is changing weekly, my lips strip and shed when they feel like it, I have dry mouth most days (eating is harder because some foods go into my mouth and turn into a ball), my stomach is smaller so I fill up quicker, I weigh 125 lbs., and I don't look like what I used to. BUT I AM HOME BEING SPOILED BY MY SISTER AND OTHER CAREGIVERS, INSTEAD OF IN A MORGUE OR CEMETERY, SO I'LL TAKE THIS ALTERNATIVE. I GIVE THANKS THAT MY BEAUTY IS NOT DETERMINED BY MY CURRENT APPEARANCE BUT BY THE BEAUTY OF JESUS THAT EMANATES FROM ME. When I emerge looking like God's gorgeous girl, I will testify of His goodness, smile like never before, influence decision makers, change the atmosphere wherever I go, impact lives at a greater level and live life with more passion than I have ever done before. #AliveAndGettingWell #BeautyIsNotSkinDeep #GratefulToGod

Dec 9, 2017, 2:27 AM

God carried me safely through my '100 Critical Days Post Transplant'!!! What does this mean? Certain restrictions will be lifted, less doctor visits, no need for 24-hour caregivers, and I can finally go to church (wearing a mask and gloves, no hugs or handshakes). I am a 100-day old baby being carried by the Lord, watching my body transform, experiencing new sleep patterns and different taste buds. I give God all the glory and praise!!!! Thanks to everyone who helped me through this season so that I could get to this milestone.

Fitting Facebook Post to Summarize 2017

Dec 31, 2017, 9:54 PM

My highlights for 2017—The year I conquered in many ways, the year I found love that I never knew existed in people I never knew cared for me, the year cancer confronted me and I beat it, the year I was rejected by people I thought would be there even in the smallest ways, the year I saw practical Christianity on full display, the year strangers reached out to me and poured in like I could not believe, the year I knew for sure I was at the right church, the year I finally felt like I had spiritual covering, the year I did not work but God took care of every need, the year I felt God's affirmation and explanation of the path He allowed my life to take, the year it all made sense, the year I feel destiny colliding with purpose, the year I was most intentional about making God proud, making Him known and making others realize life is still a gift no matter how bad things may be. #2017BestNine #2017WasABlessedYear #2017GodKeptMe #2017ISawJesusInPeople #2017IReleaseAndLetGo #2017IAmGrateful

ACTION ITEM

Visit Be The Match website to get information on how easy it is to be added to the donor registry. https://bethematch.org/

Visit MedLine Plus https://medlineplus.gov/ for more information on bone marrow transplants.

CHAPTER 21

Blessings In Disguise

rior to dealing with cancer, I would never have known that significant blessings and life lessons could accompany the diagnosis. Apart from the obvious blessings such as a great medical team, the right treatment plan, a supportive family and people who prayed for me constantly, I realized that several other things blessed my life tremendously. As each situation occurred and I recognized it for what it was, it enabled my perspective to be adjusted. **Cancer taught me that I should not prematurely label a situation as a devastating dilemma because it could be the delivery of blessings and destiny in disguise.**

Reunions with Childhood Friends

My heart squealed with delight each time I was visited by someone from my childhood and teenage years. People travelled from near and far to share the gift of their presence with me at the hospital and in my home. These reunions were meaningful because in most cases, I had not seen these people in over 20 years. I am grateful they took the time to pay me a visit, share memories and pray out loud so that I could hear what was being prayed for.

Payments on Pause

Not being able to work and being deemed disabled meant that I qualified for certain monthly payments to be placed on pause. My insurance company gave me a waiver and student loans placed everything on hold so that I would not have to continue making either one of those payments until I recovered and started earning again.

Ravens Assigned to Feed and Take Care of Me

One of the things that really helped me get through the journey with minimal stress was that God promised that He had ravens assigned to feed and take care of me. The Lord reiterated many times that in addition to being His daughter, I was on assignment fulfilling His plan, so it was His responsibility to take care of me. I was reminded of the prophet Elijah in the Bible who was fed by ravens consistently as he went through a season in his life. In the same way, the Lord kept His word and people obeyed His instruction to either make a one-time financial gift, send a significant amount periodically or consistently to take care of a household bill. There were people who made sure I had food and groceries, even if it meant going out in the rain to bring me a bag of rice or coming late at night after Bible Study to drop off a case of water because there was none in the home.

Mommy and a few church sisters made sure I always had clothes that fit based on my size at each stage of the weight journey. At my lowest, I went down to 107 lbs. which meant that I needed all things new in the clothing and undergarment department. But then as I started to regain my weight, there were church sisters who bought and brought me clothes so that I would look and feel gorgeous, stylish and confident. I rarely had enough money to buy myself or my children nice clothes and accessories, but the Lord allowed the right people to see those needs and make the provision. Most of my new accessories are gifts from considerate, stylish ladies who know the importance of being fashionable even if one is recovering from a health challenge.

Let me make it abundantly clear that I do not hold it against anyone who could have or should have stepped up to do their part in assisting me and my family as we went through the cancer journey. People are not obligated to come alongside and provide tangible or intangible assistance if they choose not to do so. My faith in God and His ability to take care of me reiterated what I already knew deep inside. Not everyone was or is supposed to play a role in this process because the trusted people received God-approved authorization. It is possible that the Lord deliberately excluded some people because He knew they would have taken the glory for themselves. God knows who He can trust to be His hands and heart extended and He also knows that some gifts come with tainted strings attached. There are people who will help but will also hold it over your head forever and make a show to others for the sake of bragging. God knew that not everyone could be trusted to walk this journey with us, take care of the necessary needs and do it with discretion, respect, grace and have no desire for repayment. I am grateful that God hand-picked the right people who would willingly, lovingly and consistently agree to do whatever He asked them to do on our behalf.

Shift in Perspective (Low Tolerance for Foolishness and Pettiness)

It's amazing how fighting for one's life will quickly place things and people in proper perspective, which leaves little or no room for foolishness and pettiness. Let me make it plain without coming across as crude, cold or caustic in my comments. Life continues while the cancer journey is taking place, which means one must choose what to focus on and how to expend emotional energy. Therefore, there is a low tolerance or desire to entertain trivial (or trash) talk, petty people's perceptions, or inconsequential interactions. Going through a cancer journey and recovery means that one must safeguard their own emotions in order to limit stressors. Consequently, it may require distancing and severing all ties with people, places and positions (temporarily or permanently). Some things and certain people are detrimental to maintaining good mental health and a safe environment. Interact with people according to wisdom with the goal of minimizing negativity and stressful people.

Vlogging

The year before the diagnosis, I planned to set up a home studio so that I could regularly record video blogs on various subject matters. From time to time, I recorded and posted inspirational and thought-provoking videos for social media. But when I started the cancer journey, the Lord prompted me to share my observations and experiences via videos. At first it was very difficult to get comfortable with those instructions because it would require revealing raw, real moments. I was the kind of lady who didn't even go to the grocery store without a little makeup and a decent looking outfit. Self-image was and still is important to me, so can you imagine how this grown-up girly girl felt when I had to accept that God wanted me to share videos while I looked like a hot mess???!!!! I was not pleased or excited. I threw a grown-up girl tantrum and made my displeasure known. "Who do you think I am that I should put myself out there for the cruel comments from people who have no compassion? "Yu tek mi fi popishow?" I said in my Jamaican dialect. (*Translation*, "Do you take me for a show?") Anyway, once I calmed my prideful self down several notches, I remembered songs I sang in worship that pretty much told the Lord to use me whenever and however He wanted. I realized that this cancer journey wasn't just about me, so each time He nudged me to do a video, I obeyed the Lord's instructions for the benefit of the many people who needed to see and hear what it was really like. Thankfully these videos have become a source of encouragement, inspiration and a shift in perspective for cancer patients. Several times I have been told that a patient felt like giving up prematurely but when they watched my videos, they received help and hope to continue fighting for themselves. I have also been told that people learned so much about the process, pitfalls and painful parts of the journey, so now they know how to assist and interact more appropriately with someone dealing with cancer.

Closer Relationship with God and the Faith Gym

To me, the best blessing in disguise was the intimacy I developed in my relationship with the Lord and the faith that grew daily. I've always had a good relationship as a Christ-follower. Like every other Christian committed to living a lifestyle of faith and obedience to the Lord, I have had my ups and downs. I accepted the Lord as my personal Savior when I was 9 years old and was baptized by my father, the late Rev. Eric Lewis, when I was 10 years old. I wanted to wait a year to see if I was really saved this time. (Remember that I previously indicated that as a young child, I frequently went to the altar for salvation trying to get rid of guilt, shame and confusion?) Anyway, I have been a Christian for most of my life. I backslid a few times (no shame in admitting that) but could never really get away from the grace, mercy, forgiveness or love of God. Each time I stupidly stumbled or walked with my eyes wide open into sin, He kept pulling me back. After daddy died, I lost my faith in God and took on a cynical mindset that God is going to do whatever He wants to, so why bother living by faith. But through the years, as my relationship with God grew through the application of His Word and the way He loved me unconditionally, so did my faith.

Nothing tests a person's faith like having to believe the Word of God for oneself in a health crisis. It is easy to pray and believe for others, but it is a totally different level of faith that is required when one must take their own measure of faith and apply it during a crucial health challenge. Add to that, the loss of regular income to take care of the daily financial obligations and that takes things to another level that demands total trust and reliance on God. Not only must one have faith to believe for healing, recovery and strength, but faith must be exercised to believe God for food, clothing, shelter and everything else that is needed to live well. I refer to this as being in the "faith gym" because it means pushing myself to exercise my faith each week like an athlete lifting weights and running on a treadmill to accomplish fitness goals.

Watching the ways in which God honored my faith was the best blessing that resulted from the cancer journey. As I write this, I am still not working in a full-time capacity making a decent income with great benefits (and it's not for lack of trying). I have submitted several applications to companies where I believe I have the necessary qualifications and experience. However, I have not been accepted at any of those jobs. I must pay for very expensive private health insurance and take care of a household. For me, I consider my current life experience as being in the faith gym every week because I must rely on God to provide consistently, especially when unexpected things occur, like a car repair, children's school/extracurricular activities, etc. As a result, my faith in God grows in those moments of uncertainty when all I can do is trust that He is aware of every need and will provide in a timely manner.

Reflecting on all the blessings that accompanied the cancer and transplant journey caused me to praise passionately the first Sunday I returned to my place on the choir at The River of Life Christian Center. As we sang and danced, my choir members left their positions to hug me. Before I realized what was happening, my worship leader, LaRue Howard, left center stage, came to me, took my hand and began marching with me across the stage so that the congregation could see that I was back. A fellow choir sister took my other hand and together they raised my hands as we took a victory lap as the congregation rejoiced. Little did I know that a professional photographer, Lia Epps, was in the congregation and captured the unplanned moment of public praise to God for taking me through the journey.

ACTION ITEM

Go to **Shannan Lewis' Conquering Cancer Journey** (https://www.youtube.com/watch?v=bkxwgV4atPk&list=PLCGMd-Dzo2F3YOcvYF_XEeMpjNerNTCs4d) **on YouTube and watch the videos.**

Please SHARE these videos with others who could benefit from my transparent truths

CHAPTER 22

People's Perception

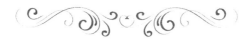

B e open to the strong possibility that many people will view you differently during and after your recovery. Their perception may cause them to treat you in a different way as though you have lost value as an individual. Some people may admire you for undergoing the process and coming out as a survivor. However, many people will tend to regard you with tentative hesitation and trepidation as it pertains to your abilities going forward. If you are blessed and fortunate to continue living a decent "normal" life after you have gone through cancer treatment, keep in mind that some people will wonder if the cancer will return and even consider how much time you have left. Sadly, life experience has taught many people to regard cancer as an automatic death sentence, so folks subconsciously prepare for the worse and carry that expectation in their minds even if they do not verbalize it.

The other perception that may change is in the area of your professional life. Prior to being diagnosed, I had two professional positions – University Admissions Counselor and Adjunct Professor. However, due to the nature of my roles, primarily the need to be physically present on campus, the university was not able to keep me employed for an extended period or hold on to my position. The recovery journey was expected to be long which meant business needs had to be planned for. In fact, I participated in the interview process for my admissions counselor replacement from my hospital bed. My full-time employment ended a few months after treatment. Add another year for the bone marrow transplant journey and that meant I was unable to work in a full-time job for about two years. I had to consider the strong possibility that even though I had an impressive resume which boasted excellent qualifications, a bachelor's degree and a master's degree, as well as many years of experience in various fields, hiring managers who knew anything about my recent journey could choose not to take a chance on me. Even though I am aware that laws protect the disabled (anyone who has gone through the cancer journey is automatically deemed disabled), I could not ignore the possibility that if hiring managers knew that I had dealt with cancer, they could choose not to hire me. After each rejection from positions that I thought would be a good fit for me, I had to grapple with the possibility that some hiring managers may see me as a risky hire or a potential liability.

In other situations, some people may not invite or include you to participate in certain activities for fear that you will become a bother, burden or their responsibility if you have any limitations or restrictions. People may not realize that this is their subconscious response to you, so don't be surprised if you are not informed about adventures, excursions or exciting social events. It's not that people don't want to have you join in the fun, but it could be that people no longer view you as someone allowed to have fun. Dealing with and overcoming a cancer diagnosis means people may perceive you as "damaged goods", and as a result, interact from a place of uncertainty, fear and mistrust.

Granted, their concerns may be valid depending on your recovery journey and new normal if you are still undergoing treatment, or after the process has ended. Try to not take it personally if people give you the impression that you are no longer worth of their inclusion, investment or invitation. People mean well but usually operate from a place of caution, convenience and comfort.

To counteract negative feelings that may arise as a result of the way people view and treat you, choose to remember who you are NOW, not who you used to be. While it is true that you are still the same person, recognize and own the fact that you have transformed and evolved in many ways. Chemo drugs and high dose medication changed many things about the way your body looks, feels and functions. The emotional adjustment of undergoing a cancer diagnosis and treatments also changes your entire perspective on many things. Accept that you are a different person now than you were the day before you were diagnosed.

Getting to this place of self-acceptance was (and still is) very difficult for me, because I have lived with myself for more years than the post-cancer, post-transplant self. I am no longer the same person – well, technically I am. It's still me, I am still Shannan. But the fact of the matter is that after having gone through the entire process for the past few years, I am a more settled, solid, seasoned, smart, sensible, strategic, safe, self-aware, spiritual and socially alive version of myself. I'm the best I have ever been in my entire life. This is not a statement that comes from a place of arrogance. This realization emanates like a phoenix rising from the ashes and coming up stronger, better, happier and wiser than before. It is the recognition that I went to war and came back bearing battle scars which I regard as my medals of distinction and honor. It is my acknowledgement that even if people see me differently or in a diminished capacity, I see all that I am now after having gone through the experience. I see that what was meant to disrupt and possibly destroy my life, delivered blessings and lessons that I would have never received if cancer didn't show up like an uninvited, unwanted guest.

CHAPTER 23

Call to Action

What Can Churches & Organizations Do to Support Cancer Patients and Survivors?

Before being diagnosed and walking through the cancer journey, I had very little frame of reference regarding what it was like for a cancer patient, especially someone who was actively involved in church, the community and in their organizations. Now that I have gone through the experience, I can make suggestions specifically to church and community leaders that are meant to provide more than prayers and best wishes. Each of the following may not be relevant to your situation, but I am sure you can help to effect the necessary changes within your sphere of influence.

- Change the "sick and shut-in" label used to describe patients who are bravely battling their cancer journey. Use creative, empowering, affirming words and phrases when speaking of someone dealing with a health challenge. ("Brave warrior" comes to mind as a suggestion)

- Create a cancer support group that meets in person or virtually. Being able to speak the language of cancer with others who are going through or have gone through it is essential for the psyche. It is also helpful for caregivers and children to have safe spaces where they can share freely without feeling like they are betraying their loved one by expressing their real, raw emotions.

- Adjust the focus from overseas missions' projects by also creating opportunities for local missions that assist the ones in our immediate community. Ensure that programs are in place to help take care of church members who served and contributed faithfully to the local church but are undergoing a health challenge. While it is commendable and caring to reach across the isles to donate in large quantities to foreign countries, churches and organizations should focus more heavily on taking care of the ones who have been serving in their local establishments.

- Keep people informed, in the loop, and in the know. "Out of sight, out of mind" usually means people who are dealing with a health challenge are no longer kept informed about events, members' activities and special occasions. Be intentional about keeping the brave warrior informed about things that are taking place at church, in the community and in families.

- Livestream services or find other ways to share with the brave warriors who are not able to attend church. Technology offers various options which could ensure that the sick is still able to see and hear what is happening at church.

- Provide reasonable accommodation in work and church environments to allow the brave warrior to have a sense of comfort based on their individual needs. Not every person will be willing to take the initiative and make the request for accommodation, therefore leadership should ask pertinent questions in order to anticipate those needs.

- Employers should adjust their expectations regarding the person's quality vs. quantity of work. If the brave warrior is able to return to gainful employment, those in leadership should lay aside biases and lowered expectations about potential job performance. Granted, it is possible that the person's ability to work in the same position may be different because, let's face it, they are different in some ways. If there are no specific areas of disability, then chances are the brave warrior will be able to handle and excellently execute most tasks. The speed and quantity of output may not be the same, but if there are few limitations, that person will be able to work well in most job situations.

CHAPTER 24

Planning to Live Long and Well

As promised at the beginning of this "interactive dialog", I wanted to use this book to help prepare you and your loved ones for what the cancer journey may include. I wrote this for those who could use the real, raw information from someone who went through it, conquered it and is now on the other side of it. I don't know how much longer I have to live on this earth, but my promise to God, myself, my family and my future is to live each day with intention, striving to do everything that I was designed to do before I even arrived on this planet.

I recently heard someone say something to this effect, "Just because I had cancer and I'm now living cancer-free, it's not something I want to talk about or be reminded of all the time." My ears and heart perked up when I heard those words because I could relate. Don't get me wrong; it's not that I am feeling ungrateful or tired of talking about the cancer chapter of my life story. It's just that I have had to accept that it is and will always be a part of my life story. Dealing with a cancer diagnosis means navigating a new normal in many areas of life, especially if the treatment process was lengthy and laborious. It doesn't mean I don't enjoy sharing my story whenever the opportunity presents itself, but it does mean that each day I am reminded of the journey in various ways that I don't necessarily want to always discuss. **Your cancer diagnosis will always be a chapter of your story, but it doesn't have to be the main narrative of your life.**

It's been two years since all that transpired and honestly, I have no regrets because the cancer journey was a devastating disruption that was really the delivery of lessons, blessings and destiny in disguise. Only God knows why He allowed me to walk this path instead of using other means to accomplish the same results. Was a cancer diagnosis the worst thing that ever happened to me? No, not at all. I know what that "worst thing" was but even that does not define or diminish me, and neither does the cancer journey. It was simply a chapter in my life story that had to be lived and I chose to allow it to unfold in ways that made God proud, made me stronger and made my fellow citizens see that it is possible to walk through a cancer journey inspiring, informing and impacting lives in positive ways.

I still plan to live well!! I'm still a young lady at heart and youthful in years. I still intend to accomplish everything I wrote down on a PowerPoint presentation slide while in the hospital when I decided and determined that cancer was not going to end my life story prematurely. Today, I have that list of reminders in my bedroom so that each time I see it, I remember to live with purpose and passion. There is no need to wait on the ideal circumstances to live life well, it simply is a matter of choosing to do so each day. My hope is that you will wake up every day and make that decision regardless of the circumstances that you face.

The cancer diagnosis delivered destiny in disguise, lessons that needed to be learned and loads of love from people that I never knew cared so deeply.

Here's to the rest of my life. I am eager to live it to the best of my ability, blooming where I am planted and making God proud in the process.

References

American Cancer Society. 2019. "Chemotherapy". Retrieved from: https://www.cancer.org/treatment/treatments-and-side-effects/treatment-types/chemotherapy.html

Be The Match. 2017. "Other Diseases". Retrieved from: https://bethematch.org/patients-and-families/about-transplant/blood-cancers-and-diseases-treated-by-transplant/other-diseases/

Cancer Treatment Centers of America. 2019. "Leukemia stages". Retrieved from: https://www.cancercenter.com/cancer-types/leukemia/stages

Cirino, Erica. 2018, April 10. "What Are the Benefits of Hugging?" [Blog post] *Healthline.* Retrieved from: https://www.healthline.com/health/hugging-benefits#1

CV SkinLabs Team. 2009, May 3. "The Big Hair Scare: Is It Safe To Shave And Wax During Cancer Treatment?" [Blog post] *CV Skinlabs Blog.* Retrieved from: https://cvskinlabs.com/the-big-hair-scare-is-it-safe-to-shave-and-wax-during-cancer-treatment/

Ellis, Vesphew. 1964. "Let Me Touch Him". *Hymnary.* Retrieved from: https://hymnary.org/text/let_me_touch_him_let_me_touch_jesus

Good Reads. 2019. "Quotes by Woody Allen". Retrieved from: https://www.goodreads.com/quotes/16117-sex-is-the-most-fun-you-can-have-without-laughing

Huneck, Jessica. 2020, February 15. "Compare Whole Life Vs. Term Life." *Trusted Choice.* Retrieved from: https://www.trustedchoice.com/life-insurance/coverage-basics/whole-life-vs-term-life/

Lee, Tiffany Arbuckle, Luke Harry Walker Sheets, and Christa Nicole Wells. 2012. "Need You Now (How Many Times) Lyrics." Accessed July 18, 2020. Lyrics.com, STANDS4 LLC, 2020 https://www.lyrics.com/lyric/31055622/Plumb.

Memorial Sloan Kettering Cancer Center. 2018. "About Implanted Ports". Retrieved from: https://www.mskcc.org/cancer-care/patient-education/your-implanted-port

Mosher, Helen. 2017, January 23. "6 Reasons People Don't Buy Insurance (And Why They're Wrong)". [Blog post]. *Life Happens.* Retrieved from: https://lifehappens.org/blog/6-reasons-people-dont-buy-life-insurance-and-why-theyre-wrong/

Nordqvist, Christian. 2013, November 23. "Cold Environment Makes Cancer Grow and Spread Faster". [Blog post]. *Medical News Today.* Retrieved from: https://www.medicalnewstoday.com/articles/269266#:~:text=Humans%20with%20cancer%20are%20more,and%20promote%20their%20own%20survival.

OncoLink Team. 2018. "Women's Guide to Sexuality During And After Cancer Treatment." [Blog post].

OncoLink.Org. Retrieved from: https://www. oncolink.org/support/sexuality-fertility/sexuality/ women-s-guide-to-sexuality-during-after-cancer-treatment

Sissons, Claire. Updated 2020, June 7. 2019. "How much blood is in the human body?" *Medical News Today*. Retrieved from: https://www.medicalnewstoday.com/articles/321122

WebMD. 2019. Cancer Health Center: Retrieved from: https:// www.webmd.com/cancer/default.htm

About the Author

S hannan Lewis is a higher education professional who earned her bachelor's and master's degrees at Palm Beach Atlantic University. She was an adjunct professor and university Admissions Counselor when cancer disrupted her life. Shannan was born in Jamaica but migrated to the United States, where she has built a life in Orlando, Florida. Her ability to communicate and convey the lessons learned and blessings bestowed during the cancer journey is a love letter of sorts to the many lives that this book is meant to inform, influence, inspire and impact.

CPSIA information can be obtained
at www.ICGtesting.com
Printed in the USA
BVHW040535221220
596014BV00008B/131